My HOPE Story

Volume Three

hope✳books collaborations

Published by hope*books

2217 Matthews Township Pkwy
Suite D302
Matthews, NC 28105
www.hopebooks.com
hope*books is a division of hope*media

Printed in the United States of America

Second edition.
Paperback ISBN: 979-8-89185-431-4
Hardcover ISBN: 979-8-89185-432-1
Ebook ISBN: 979-8-89185-433-8
Library of Congress Number: 2026943842

Table of Contents

Content Warning: This book discusses experiences including suicide, sexual assault, domestic violence, and other forms of trauma. Although these topics are addressed throughout the book, the emphasis is on healing, recovery, resilience, and personal growth rather than graphic descriptions of traumatic events.

Readers are encouraged to engage with this material in a manner that supports their well-being.

Foreword
By Brian Dixon

Stories of hope do not deny pain—they carry it, and they reveal that God is present within it. The pages that follow are written from places of grief, trauma, recovery, parenting, failure, restoration, and quiet daily faithfulness. And yet, woven through every story is a steady thread: God is not absent in the darkest chapters of our lives.

As Romans 15:13 reminds us, hope is not self-generated—it is received. It is the overflow of a God who fills weary hearts with joy and peace through the power of His Spirit. These authors have not written from perfect endings but from honest journeys where God met them in suffering, silence, questions, and healing.

Within these testimonies, you will find valleys walked through, identities rebuilt, families strengthened, and faith rediscovered. You will see how God gently works not only in dramatic rescue moments but also in ordinary days—the day-in and day-out places where hope is often hardest to hold and yet most faithfully sustained.

My prayer as you read is not only that you are encouraged but that you recognize something familiar in these stories. Perhaps a moment of your own sorrow. Perhaps a season of waiting. Perhaps a reminder that God has been nearer than you realized.

Your story is not outside the reach of redemption. It is not too broken, too complicated, or too far gone. The same God who enters into these pages enters into your life with the same presence, the same mercy, and the same restoring love.

May these stories remind you that hope is not fragile— it is anchored. And it is held by the One who does not leave, does not forget, and does not give up on His people.

Sincerely,

Brian Dixon

Publisher, hope*books

About the Chapters

Chapter 1
Ramela G. Abbamontian

In this moving and faith-filled chapter, the author shares the heartbreaking journey of walking through her young daughter's cancer diagnosis during the uncertainty of the pandemic. Faced with fear, helplessness, and unimaginable pain, she learns to surrender the battle to God, cling tightly to His promises, and find strength in His presence day by day. Through the support of family, community, prayer, and countless reminders of God's faithfulness, the author discovers that even in life's darkest moments, God is able to do immeasurably more than we could ever ask or imagine. This powerful testimony offers hope to anyone facing overwhelming circumstances, reminding readers that God's presence, peace, and sustaining grace carry us through every trial.

Chapter 2
Ericka Reid

In this heartfelt and vulnerable chapter, the author shares her journey of growing up with the pain and unanswered questions surrounding an absent biological father. Through years of wrestling with feelings of abandonment, rejection, perfectionism, and fear, she discovers that her identity is not defined by who left but by the

God who chose and loved her unconditionally. With the help of counseling, prayer, self-reflection, and emotional healing, she learns to separate her worth from her father's choices and embrace freedom, forgiveness, and emotional wholeness. This powerful story reminds readers that even wounds from the past can be redeemed and that true healing begins when we recognize we are deeply loved, chosen, and never abandoned by God.

Chapter 3
Stacey Gawthrop

In this heartfelt chapter, the author shares the deeply personal journey of walking through financial uncertainty, unexpected life transitions, and learning to trust God when His plans looked nothing like her own. What began as years of praying for her husband's dream career led their family into seasons of waiting, surrender, and overwhelming dependence on God's provision. Through closed doors, unanswered questions, and moments of desperation, she discovered that God's faithfulness often unfolds in ways far greater than we can imagine when we loosen our grip on our own expectations. This powerful testimony reminds readers that even in the hardest seasons, God is quietly working behind the scenes, turning uncertainty into unimaginable blessing and teaching us to live with open hands and surrendered hearts.

Chapter 4
Katherine Freeman

This chapter shares a mother's journey of learning to surrender her adult son to God while walking alongside his struggle with schizophrenia and suicidal thoughts. Through years of fear, exhaustion, and striving to "fix" what she could not control, she gradually discovered the peace that comes from trusting the Lord's care and presence. As God renewed her faith, she learned to pursue healing for her own heart, embrace community, and rediscover joy and purpose in the midst of ongoing uncertainty. This story offers hope and encouragement to caregivers and families navigating the challenges of serious mental illness.

Chapter 5
Lindsay Koach

This chapter shares a powerful testimony of healing, surrender, and spiritual renewal through a difficult health journey. As the author faced hypothyroidism, hormonal imbalance, and emotional exhaustion, she discovered that true healing required not only physical changes but also a deeper trust in God and a renewed relationship with Him. Through gratitude, healthier living, prayer, and releasing her need for control, she experienced transformation in her mind, body, and spirit. Her story encourages readers to seek God's guidance in seasons of suffering, trust His process, and find hope in His faithfulness and peace.

Chapter 6
Melanie Wamoff

This chapter reflects on the author's realization, shaped by painful college roommate experiences, that close relationships don't happen automatically—they require intentional, Christ-centered effort. Inspired by a family who modeled genuine sibling friendship rooted in Scripture, she and her husband chose to parent with purpose, shaping how their children viewed one another through everyday conversations and biblical truth. Over time, those small, consistent choices helped their children grow into close friends who genuinely enjoy and support one another. The chapter carries a deeply personal hope that God can transform ordinary homes into places of lasting unity, love, and friendship when they are grounded in His Word.

Chapter 7
Anna Gall

This chapter tells the story of a deeply painful experience of sexual assault, confusion, and shame, and how it led to a long journey of healing, repentance, and rediscovering identity in Christ. The author describes the immediate emotional and spiritual impact of the trauma, including fear, isolation, and misplaced coping responses but also a powerful moment of conviction where she turns back to God in repentance and begins seeking help through counseling and faith. Over time, she rebuilds her life through therapy, spiritual grounding, forgiveness, and practical steps of personal growth, learning to see herself through the "mirror" of God's Word rather than through guilt or the opinions of others. Ultimately, the chapter becomes a testimony of restoration, showing how God's grace, forgiveness, and truth lead her from brokenness into resilience, renewed identity, and hope.

Chapter 8

Elisa Rendon

This chapter is a deeply personal testimony of moving from severe mental illness, trauma, and repeated suicide attempts into healing and hope through a restored relationship with Jesus Christ. The author shares how seasons of brokenness, isolation, and medical diagnosis eventually gave way to an understanding that she was never abandoned by God, even in her darkest moments. Through Scripture, motherhood, and gradual spiritual renewal, she experienced Christ's unconditional love and forgiveness in a way that reshaped her identity and brought stability to her life. Ultimately, the chapter emphasizes that nothing can separate us from God's love and that redemption and new life are possible through Jesus, even after profound suffering.

Chapter 9

Noemi Rivas

This chapter follows a deeply personal journey through grief, beginning with the author's lifelong sensitivity to pain and early coping mechanism of using laughter to mask emotional wounds. As an adult, that coping strategy breaks down, and she is faced with profound loss when her father becomes critically ill and passes away while she is newly married and pregnant. In the midst of overwhelming sorrow, she learns to lean into prayer, Scripture, community, and God's presence as her primary sources of strength and comfort. Ultimately, the experience reshapes her understanding of grief, revealing a hope anchored in faith, gratitude, and the belief that God meets her in both suffering and healing.

Chapter 10
Charlotte Hubrich

In this deeply personal chapter, the author shares her journey of chasing lifelong dreams and discovering that success and approval could never fill the emptiness in her heart. Through years of striving to prove her worth as an actress, she experienced disappointment, anxiety, and emotional exhaustion before finally surrendering her ambitions to God. With honesty and vulnerability, the author reflects on how God gently renewed her mind, restored her peace, and redirected her life toward lasting joy, purpose, and contentment in Christ. Her story is a powerful reminder that true fulfillment comes not from achievement, but from accepting God's unconditional love and trusting His plans above our own.

Immeasurably More: Strength for the Journey Through a Child's Cancer Diagnosis

By Ramela G. Abbamontian

"NOW TO HIM WHO IS ABLE TO DO IMMEASURABLY MORE THAN ALL WE ASK OR IMAGINE, ACCORDING TO HIS POWER THAT IS AT WORK WITHIN US, TO HIM BE GLORY IN THE CHURCH AND IN CHRIST JESUS THROUGHOUT ALL GENERATIONS, FOR EVER AND EVER! AMEN. "
—*EPHESIANS 3:20-21, NIV*

"Is there a chance I could die?" my 11-year-old uttered as she looked at me with tear-glistened eyes and a gentle head tilt seeking her mama's reassurance.

"No!" was my resolute reply, though I knew the honest answer to that question was unspeakably, "Yes."

It had barely been two hours since we'd rushed to the Emergency Room. I was walking back to Lily's room from the restroom when I heard, "Are you Lily's mom? We need to talk to you." The words interrupted my thoughts, and I looked up at the COVID-mandated masked doctor standing in the sterile hospital hallway. I nodded and turned towards Lily's room. "No, this way please," the doctor pointed to the opposite end of the hallway. My heart skipped a beat, and my chest tightened.

"But ... my husband ... he's not here ... he was sent home. They told us that there are still many more tests to run before we get any answers."

"That's OK. You can FaceTime him." Facetime? That's odd. My heart skipped another beat.

By the time we got to the small corner room, three others had joined us. More masked strangers. I couldn't read their barricaded expressions. We crowded into the stuffy room, each of us taking a corner recliner. I FaceTimed my husband, "Honey, can you go someplace private? They need to talk to us." I fumbled as I positioned his face up against the pot on the small table. Settling into the seat, pen in position, I flipped to an empty page in my notebook, ready to record what the doctor had to say about the cause of the 5-day, relentless fever and incessant abdominal pains that eventually brought us to the ER. Gallstones? Pancreatic issues? Appendicitis? The doctor began talking fast, and I scribbled quickly to keep up, trying to record her every word.

Suspicious for cancer.

Wait, what? I looked up, then looked down at what I had just written.

Suspicious for cancer.

Maybe I had misunderstood. "I'm sorry, doctor, what did you just say?" I looked up again from my scribbles.

She elaborated, "The scan showed masses in the chest, abdomen, and near the right kidney. They are suspicious for cancer."

No, no, no. That's not why we rushed her to the ER. It was a "tummy ache" and a fever. When the pediatrician had called with lab results and asked us to rush to the Emergency Room of the Children's Hospital, she had clearly said, "It's not life-threatening, but we need to know why her white blood count is so high." No, not cancer. I wasn't here for a cancer diagnosis.

I looked down at my husband's face in the tilted screen on the table. "Jimmy, did you hear what she just said?" My husband mumbled something.

Lightheaded and disoriented, I could barely make out the rest of what the doctor said—something about having to stay overnight for more testing. *Suspicious for cancer.* I was still trying to process these piercing words that had just stabbed my heart.

Everyone left the room, except the social worker. My body went limp, and I melted to the floor, buried my face into the seat, and began to sob uncontrollably. I couldn't hear what the social worker was saying. *God? Where are you, God?* was all I could utter. All I heard on repeat was "suspicious for cancer."

Clinging to His Promises and Character

We settled into Lily's new room on the oncology floor. Since Jimmy's return to the hospital immediately after our call, we hadn't left our daughter's side. Stolen glances were all that we could exchange as we tried to process the pain and confusion without letting Lily know what the doctor had said.

We were given a more extensive report the next day after the radiologist had reviewed the scans more thoroughly. Jimmy and I were taken to yet another small and stuffy room. The oncologist rolled in a computer and began matter-of-factly to click through screen after screen, pointing to the cloudy patches visible in her abdomen and to the "innumerable" metastatic masses that had found their home in her precious lungs. She said the biopsy would reveal what kind of cancer she had as well as additional details. Jimmy and I looked at each other—we already knew we were dealing with seemingly insurmountable odds.

We didn't know how to share this news with our little girl, so we asked the head nurse to explain what was happening to Lily, as we assumed she had done this countless number of times and would be better able to deliver the news with compassion and neutrality. We sat on the couch as the nurse knelt beside Lily's hospital bed. She didn't use the word "cancer," and in a long, indirect explanation, described the need for treatment. I did my best to hold back tears and fixed my eyes on my little girl, waiting for a reaction. But there was none. She sat, silent and still. I wasn't sure she'd been able to make sense of the nurse's somewhat convoluted explanation.

After the nurse left the room, I gently sat down on Lily's bed, so as not to disturb the awkward silence. Her next question revealed that she'd understood *exactly* what the nurse had explained. "Is there a chance that I could die?"

"No!" —the only acceptable answer; the only one she, and we, could handle in that moment.

Lily eventually fell asleep, and I made my way to the window overlooking the flickering LA skyline. I dumped my numb body onto the uncomfortable convertible couch, facing the window, and as quietly as I could, released the tears I had held back for over twenty-four hours. The abrasive hospital tissue didn't offer much comfort. My tears saturated the pillow. I desperately wanted to drown out the replay of the doctor's words still echoing in my hollow and numb body. Blinking through blurry and weary eyes, I fidgeted with my phone, looking for the Bible meditation app that I loved and had relied on so many times in difficult moments. I desperately needed the anchor of God's Word. Finally finding a meditation for "hope," I placed the phone under my pillow, rested my head on His promises, cried in my Father's lap, and eventually fell asleep in His comforting arms.

The next two days were a frenzy of scans, labs, port placement, and a biopsy—a frenzy I was familiar with from when I was diagnosed with breast cancer. But hiding our fears behind our reassuring smiles, we prayed for Lily and sent her off into the procedure room to place the port and do a biopsy.

Jimmy and I grabbed some food and settled into the cafeteria booth, facing each other for the first time and trying to grasp what had transpired in the last day and a half. How did the quiet and slow pace of the pandemic's first month of lockdown—filled with sleeping in, Zoom classes, daily family meals, dog walks in the neighborhood—now lead us into this unexpected hurricane of uncertainty and fear? A flood of jumbled words tumbled out as as we retraced her excruciating abdominal pains, a relentless fever, the unemotional words of the ER doctor, the horrific scan results ...

"I can't imagine losing her," Jimmy muttered as he wiped tears from his eyes—it was the first time I'd ever seen my husband cry.

Just then, suddenly, an incomprehensible strength surged from within me, and I blurted out, "Wait, Jimmy! What do we know about God? This is when our faith comes in. What do we know about Him? Our faith is for moments like this!" One by one, counting on my fingers, I began to list everything we knew to be true about our Heavenly Father:

He knows us.

He loves us.

This doesn't surprise Him.

He loves Lily even more than we do.

He has a plan for her life.

He is sovereign.

He is trustworthy.

He is faithful.

He will walk us through this.

Despite the lump in our throats, there, in the hospital's cold cafeteria, we turned our gaze to our Father—opening up the ache in our hearts and offering to the Lord our honest and fervent prayer: I reminded God how He had been faithful to lead me to Psalm 16 two days after my own diagnosis, when I had begged Him to give me some comfort and direction. Now, even more than then, I ardently prayed for another sign of hope to cling to. "In Jesus' Name, Amen," we sighed, lingering for a few more moments in the Lord's presence. My phone's *ding* announced a text message from Salpi, my dear friend who had been sending numerous encouraging Bible verses since our arrival at the hospital: "Now to him who is able to do immeasurably more than all we ask or imagine, according to his power that is at work within us" (Ephesians 3:20, NIV).

Immeasurably more? We were confused. Not a verse about healing. Not a verse about being strong for the journey ahead. But a verse from the Creator of the universe that He was going to do abundantly more than our expectations.

We were confused, but we accepted the promise in faith. We needed to see His "immeasurably more" work unfold. We did not understand, but we chose to believe.

Surrendering the Battle to the Lord

After having reviewed the numerous scans, I had turned to the doctor and asked her not to give me the prognosis—having held the lengthy and dismal pathology results in my hands, I knew the Goliath that we were facing. What good would it do to fill my mind with more data? Contrary to my nature, I refused to research anything—I didn't look up numbers or statistics, the progression of the disease, chemotherapy side effects, the population most commonly impacted, etc. I also requested that well-meaning family and friends send me encouraging Bible verses, instead of information about the disease or anything else that would cloud my mind. Familiar with the immense mental stamina needed for aggressive cancer treatment, I did not want any non-essential information taking up space in my limited mental real estate. That space was reserved for Truth—for *His* promises.

It felt like I was blindly going into battle with an enemy I didn't know well. But my Heavenly Father reminded me, "Do not be afraid or discouraged because of this vast army. For the battle is not yours, but God's" (2 Chronicles 20:15b, NIV).

Three days after the ER visit, still reeling from Lily's diagnosis, waiting at the hospital for treatment plans that had not been set yet, I woke up one morning with an angry battle cry, "I will fight for her! I will fight for her!" But then the sweet, gentle voice of my Heavenly Father reminded me again that *He* is already fighting for her, and I just need to rest in that assurance. A few hours later, the Lord confirmed this with a text from a friend: "The Lord will fight for you; you need only to be still" (Exodus 14:14, NIV).

I surrendered to Him.

Through tear-stricken words, I also surrendered my daughter to the Lord, knowing full well that her life was in His hands. *Lord, if you are going to take her from me, then I am trusting that you will walk me through that.* Only He knew the number of her days; I had no control over that. What was required of me was my faithfulness. I remembered how the Lord had walked me through my cancer journey seven years prior, so I repeated David's words, "The Lord who rescued me from the paw of the lion and the paw of the bear will rescue me from the hand of this Philistine" (1 Samuel 17:37, NIV).

Guarding my mind was not easy. It was a battle strategy that required constantly, moment-by-moment, capturing any destructive thoughts and replacing them with His promises and His truth. Each time the mental battlefield raged—fear, uncertainty, and worry colliding together to overwhelm me and destroy my peace—I fought back with the truth of who God is, remembering that, "We demolish arguments and every pretension that sets itself up against the knowledge of God, and we take captive every thought to make it obedient to Christ" (2 Corinthians 10:5, NIV). Rather than allowing myself to rehearse the hopeless scenarios, I deliberately chose to repeat the truth about His character and promises: He is good. His plans for us are good. He knows the big picture. He goes ahead of us.

In this constant battle to guard my mind, I recalled the Apostle Paul's instructive words: "Finally, brothers and sisters, whatever is true, whatever is noble, whatever is right, whatever is pure, whatever is lovely, whatever is admirable—if anything is excellent or praiseworthy— think about these things" (Philippians 4:8, NIV). I took this comforting command literally, running back to Jesus, to God's promises, and to the character of God; I fixed my mind on His goodness and the experiences of His past provision in my life through good and difficult times. I kept choosing gratitude over fear; hope over despair; the truth of His word over the scepter of the terrible diagnosis.

Giving and Receiving Presence

ER visits between chemotherapy sessions became our sad routine: Lily's fever would spike to 100.4, we'd call it in, and then rush to the hospital within the hour to ensure Lily didn't have an infection. Labs and cultures were taken, and then it was a waiting game. It was always unpredictable when we'd be cleared for discharge.

This time, we had been at the hospital for four days. Four very long days with constant nightly interruptions to measure her blood pressure, check her temperature, get labs, and adjust IV lines. Four mornings of waking up with anticipation to see if her numbers from the labs taken overnight looked promising, and, "Maybe today we can go home, Mama?" COVID restrictions imposed an isolation that felt like imprisonment. While we had each other, both my daughter and I longed for the rest of our family, with Lily especially missing her sisters, Grace and Ella.

Finally, we headed home! The freeway stretched into the horizon, teasing us with how far we still had to go. I started to recount all the blessings of this last hospital stay.

"Lily, I'm so grateful for so many things with this visit: your cultures remained negative for 48 hours. Your blood counts went up. Your fever subsided and didn't spike again. Our nurse was wonderful and ...." Unexpectedly and rather abruptly, an intrusive thought disrupted this moment of deep thanksgiving, reminding me of previous inpatient hospital stays that had been very difficult. Guilt replaced thanksgiving so quickly, as I started remembering all my failings as a mother aloud: "You had painful abdominal pains, and I couldn't do anything. You were shaking uncontrollably, and I just held you but couldn't calm you. I got impatient with you because I felt so helpless. Oh, Lily, I remember those days, and I felt so helpless. I couldn't ..."

"Mom!" she blurted out, interrupting me before I uttered another regret, "Your *presence* helped!"

I was silent for several seconds, not knowing how to respond to this deep wisdom from my now-12-year-old.

Presence. That's all she had wanted.

She didn't need me to fix anything. She didn't need me to solve problems. She just needed me to *be*. She just needed *Mom*.

As this thought lingered in my mind for the next few days, I was also reminded of God's presence. Admittedly, I frequently pray for God to take my problems away or to solve them, probably because, as a parent, that's what I think I need to do with the situations my children face. But God doesn't promise to answer my prayers in the ways that I ask of Him, but He does promise me His *presence*. "The Lord himself goes before you and will be with you; he will never leave you nor forsake you. Do not be afraid; do not be discouraged" (Deuteronomy 31:8, NIV).

When I paused to consider this, I realized that the assurance of His presence was what I needed most of all. This life is hard. This journey of walking my daughter through her toughest battle was hard beyond words. But to know that, no matter the outcome, the Creator of the universe—our Heavenly Father—promises to walk this life with me because He cares for me? That truth humbled me to no end, and it still does.

So, in the midst of an unimaginable journey, pandemic lockdown, multiple ER rushes, chemotherapy side effects, and balancing time with my two other daughters, I kept reminding myself to sit in His holy presence. Sometimes I would read His Word, and the Holy Spirit would highlight a verse for me. Other times, a friend would text a verse at the perfect moment, and I would sit with it—even scribbling it on our hospital room's whiteboard—such as, "Have I not commanded you? Be strong and courageous. Do not be afraid; do not be discouraged, for the Lord your God will be with you wherever you go" (Joshua 1:9, NIV). Every time Lily would head into yet another scan, I would sit in the corner of the room with my prayer journal and talk to God, shielding my mind against any thoughts of a negative outcome. But I felt His presence most powerfully when I would write the Caring Bridge entries to update family and friends. As I reviewed the events that had transpired since the last entry, the Holy Spirit would reveal God's presence in the details. Writing the updates and giving glory and thanksgiving to God drew me closer to my Heavenly Father and reminded me that He truly does carry us.

The more I sat in His presence, the more I began to see His fingerprints everywhere and every day. I called them God-incidences. For example, our nurse for the very first chemotherapy session was a delightful young woman by the name of Victoria, who attentively tended to Lily's every need, tenderly managing her pain and nausea. She also patiently—because I ask a lot of questions—gave me the hour-long tutorial for "newly diagnosed" patients, including how to administer an injection 24 hours after we returned home. The information was overwhelming, and I couldn't believe that's where we were: my daughter was fighting metastatic cancer, and I was her caregiver. Catching a glimpse of my tears, Victoria paused to encourage me, reminding me to "lean on God." Her words and her comforting presence brought me peace, the kind that "transcends all understanding" (Philippians 4:7, NIV). She mentioned that she was studying at a Christian university and her dad was a pastor. I then heard the Holy Spirit's sudden but soft whisper, "Ramela! Her name is Victoria. Consider it for a moment." I paused, caught off guard. Victoria? What does Victoria have to do with anything? Then it hit me: victorious! My Heavenly Father, on Lily's *first* day of implementing the battle plan, was giving me a sign of victory. I didn't know what that would look like, and, of course, I was praying for complete healing, but I knew that no matter what, she would be victorious in Him.

Presence became an anchor for us: God's presence, the presence of a loving community, the presence of kind, comforting nurses. And for Lily, the presence of her sisters, Grace and Ella, which she craved as she was often away from home. For most of her cancer journey, any time something happened, Lily reached out to her older sister, Grace, as her first source of support. Lily would simply report, "Grace, I have to do another blood transfusion," or, "Grace, I have to stay at the hospital for one more night," and at the other end, her sister's soothing words were, "Oh, my baby," and then they'd sit in silence for several minutes before the conversation changed to the next Marvel movie we were going to watch as soon as we got home. While I sometimes wished Lily would provide Grace with more details, I realized that she was simply seeking presence in that connective silence.

Creating a Community of Support and Prayer

After that first week at the hospital, where they had to run every test imaginable—countless labs, brain MRI, bone scan, bone marrow biopsy, genetic testing, to name just a few—we were finally headed home. To lift Lily's spirits, I had asked a couple of dear friends to gather a few of Lily's school friends for a surprise drive-by show of support. Pandemic restrictions prevented people from meeting in person, but many had started celebrating birthdays by having friends drive by, so I figured this was one way to welcome our daughter back home and surround her with some much-needed love and joy.

What her friends put together was beyond anything I imagined! It was a glorious celebration of over 60 cars adorned with posters and balloons, driving by, honking, and loudly declaring an impenetrable circle of love, community, and strength as #TeamLily. Even neighbors sat on their driveways holding up colorful signs. Throughout that first weekend home, as our minds slowly prepared for the battle we were about to face, our hearts lingered around our magical and sunny Saturday morning. Long after the parade of cars, we talked about the friends, the handmade signs, the heads popping out of sunroofs, the music in the cul-de-sac, the smiles, and the overflowing joy. Looking back at this special moment now, I realize that this drive-by procession was like a military parade—launching the warrior into battle and simultaneously welcoming the victor home (yes, before victory had even been won). It was also God keeping His promise—the first of many more to follow—to give us immeasurably more than what we had asked or imagined.

This moment was the birth of #TeamLily, the army that would carry us through some of the toughest days we were going to face. It was a reminder that even though a nasty virus tried to isolate us, the unbreakable bond of love kept us connected to one another: we were not alone in this fight; we had a loving and supportive community around us.

Soon after this, a friend from my Bible study suggested that we pray at 3:16 PM each day—a distinct reminder of God's love carrying us through. "For God so loved the world that he gave his one and only Son, that whoever believes in him should not perish but have eternal life" (John 3:16, NIV). It was so encouraging to know that so many were praying for Lily at that time of day, and sometimes, people would even wake up in the middle of the night to find the clock reading 3:16 and would immediately pray for us—and appropriately, most of Lily's chemotherapy sessions were through the night!

A friend from our community group pointed out that *Acts* 3:16 was also applicable to our current situation: "By faith in the name of Jesus, this man whom you see and know was made strong. It is Jesus' name and the faith that comes through him that has completely healed him, as you can all see" (Acts 3:16, NIV). I tucked each of these God-incidences into my heart and treasured them.

While we had an army constantly lifting us up, we also had one special cousin of mine, Diana, who was the prayer warrior staying up through each nightly chemotherapy session. We had gotten our routine down: I would text to let her know that we had settled into our room and would soon begin the pre-meds, followed by the different chemotherapy drugs, and then finishing off with post-meds and hydration. These treatment sessions varied anywhere from two to five hours, depending on the session and the specific drugs. What a gift Diana was to remind me that I was not alone! In the quiet of the night, while I tended to my daughter as the slow drip of this cocktail poisoned what we had come to call "rebel cells" in her body, I didn't feel alone; I knew that we were being carried not just by the army of prayer warriors but also, specifically, by one of its fiercest soldiers.

The Lord heard all of these prayers and gave us immeasurably more than anything we could have asked or imagined. After a brutal fourteen months, Lily rang the final bell signaling the successful end of treatment—praise God! We all breathed a deep, deep exhale.

With a heart overflowing with gratitude, I meditated on the Apostle Paul's words: "He has delivered us from such a deadly peril, and he will deliver us again. On him we have set our hope that he will continue to deliver us, as you help us by your prayers. Then many will give thanks on our behalf for the gracious favor granted us in answer to the prayers of many" (2 Corinthians 1:10-11, NIV).

This wasn't a journey I would have chosen to walk through. But it was one that profoundly changed me. When all I had was the Lord, I learned He was more than enough. It was in the difficult task of surrendering that I learned what trusting Him despite the circumstances—and the outcome—meant. My God is faithful, trustworthy, full of compassion, and always true to His promises. I thanked my beloved Heavenly Father for carrying us through in ways immeasurable.

Prayer for the Brokenhearted Mom

Heavenly Father,

I lift up my friend to you right now, who is wrestling with what she has just heard—unimaginable, devastating news. Her heart is aching in ways she didn't know were possible. Her chest feels tight, and she can barely breathe. Her eyes have cried endless tears. I lift her up into your lap, Lord, and I ask you to tend to her broken heart. Father, she doesn't know what the days ahead will be like, but remind her that you do. You are sovereign and still on your throne. She doesn't understand, but help her to trust you, Lord. Remind her that you love her child, even more than she does. Guard her heart and her mind, protect her peace, give her strength, and fill her with hope. Lord, I pray boldly for healing for her child. I know you can, and I ask that you will. Whatever the outcome, Lord, I pray for your sustaining grace to carry her through this journey. When things feel out of control, remind her that you are in control, and you only need her to be still. Draw her into your presence, Lord, so that she may be filled, and in turn be able to offer her presence to her child. Open her eyes, Lord, so she may see you in all the places and in all the details.

In the name of Jesus,

Amen.

Anchoring Practices

Here are two important practices to keep in mind as you prepare yourself for the journey:

Root Yourself in Community

Invite people into the journey, as their love, support, and prayers will carry you often. Identify a way in which you will be updating family and friends about your situation, since you won't have the time or energy to respond to individual texts and calls. You may find, as I did, that starting a Caring Bridge site was the easiest way to make sure everyone knew what was happening, what the family's needs were, and most importantly, what to pray for. Accept any support from family and friends—this is a humbling but beautiful moment of realizing that we are designed to live in community and to walk this life with one another. If friends want to bring meals, accept that. If someone offers to run your errands, take them up on it. Basically, let yourself be loved and carried by your community.

Rest in God's Presence

Ground yourself in His Word and His presence—that is our only hope. Grab a prayer journal and write down the attributes of God; record all the ways you see Him in the details; sit with the Lord and His Word; write Bible verses on the hospital whiteboard (and bring printouts to put on the walls).

Here are some Bible verses to keep close to your heart:

- "Have I not commanded you? Be strong and courageous. Do not be afraid; do not be discouraged, for the LORD your God will be with you wherever you go." (Joshua 1:9, NIV)

- "Do not be afraid or discouraged because of this vast army. For the battle is not yours, but God's." (2 Chronicles 20:15, NIV)

- "The Lord will fight for you; you need only to be still." (Exodus 14:14, NIV)

- "We demolish arguments and every pretension that sets itself up against the knowledge of God, and we take captive every thought to make it obedient to Christ." (2 Corinthians 10:5, NIV)

- "The LORD himself goes before you and will be with you; he will never leave you nor forsake you. Do not be afraid; do not be discouraged." (Deuteronomy 31:8, NIV)

And finally ...

> Now to him who is able to do immeasurably
> more than all we ask or imagine, according
> to his power that is at work within us, to him
> be glory in the church and in Christ Jesus
> throughout all generations, for ever and ever.
> Amen. (Ephesians 3:20-21, NIV)

Chapter 2

Abandoned Yet Chosen: The Absence That Didn't Define Me

By Ericka Reid

"HE HEALS THE BROKENHEARTED AND BINDS UP
THEIR WOUNDS."
—*PSALM 147:3, NIV*

"BUT YOU, GOD, SEE THE TROUBLE OF THE AFFLICTED;
YOU CONSIDER THEIR GRIEF AND TAKE IT IN HAND.
THE VICTIMS COMMIT THEMSELVES TO YOU;
YOU ARE THE HELPER OF THE FATHERLESS."
—*PSALM 10:14, NIV*

So Many Questions

I'm not sure when I first began to wonder about my biological father and ask questions about him. But I was in college when getting answers and understanding "why" he walked out of my life became much more important to me. I was a psychology major—primarily because I had questions that I needed answers to, and formally understanding human behavior somehow made sense to be able to do that. As I continued my education and pursued an advanced degree in Counseling & Development, it was around that time that I started asking my mother more pointed questions—I needed to know everything she knew about my biological father, including but not limited to their story, how and why it ended, and how I came to be; and if for no other reason, I had papers to write for my Marriage and Family Therapy class. Ironic.

My mother was able to answer a number of questions for me, including his name, age, where he was from, and approximate years of his enlistment in and discharge from the United States Navy. She told me their story and shared her hope and disappointment. All of which made me wonder even more about my biological father. What she had told me just wasn't enough. Who *was* he? What kind of person was he? Do I look like him? Do I have any of his mannerisms? Do I have brothers and sisters? Do they know about me? Are there grandparents, aunts, uncles, and cousins? There could be a whole family that I knew absolutely nothing about, and I didn't know if they even knew I existed. I suppose I could have made more of an effort to locate him ... but I didn't. Back then, a "private investigator" or "locator service" was beyond my reach. Besides, I was ok, right? I didn't need him. I had a good life. I had a mother who would shift the planets for me if she could. A family who loved me, believed in me, wanted the best for me, and would do everything they could to ensure

I had everything I needed. But there were questions they couldn't answer—that my mother could not answer.

I was about 24 when my heart finally broke, and I felt the grief of not knowing my biological father. It was all-out heartbreak. I had fully awakened to knowing my father had walked away from me, abandoned me, and never came back. And I did not, I could not understand why. Who does that to a baby who has caused no harm in the world?

What Does it Mean?

It was December, she was back home, and her Christmas baby would soon be here. I was my mama's baby from the very beginning. She was young—just 20 years old. She was enlisted in the U.S. Navy, stationed in northern California, and she had come home to North Carolina to have her baby. She had received an honorable discharge because, at that time, women could not remain enlisted during their pregnancy. Because she wasn't married—and that was no one's business, according to my mother and grandmother— my biological father did not come home with her, but she did hope to marry him. As it turned out, even after she returned to California, they never married.

My biological father—let's call him "bio dad"—walked away when I was two years old. I have no memory of him. What my mother has told me is that he was being discharged from the Navy and wanted to move to Los Angeles to become an actor. He didn't want to be married; there were other things he wanted to do, she had said. So off he went without so much as a look back—at least that is what I've told myself. However, my mom did say we didn't hear much from him after he left.

Some time after, she married my first stepdad, whom I also don't really remember, but I was 3 years old. My mom told me he was crazy about me, and I about him, but the marriage only lasted about a year. Then, when I was about 5 years old, she met and later married my second stepdad. That relationship lasted about 7 years. When my mother's second marriage ended, we left California and moved back to North Carolina and my mother's hometown. This time we had two other babies—my 4-year-old brother and my 6-month-old sister. I was 11 and put on the fast track for responsibility and self-sufficiency.

From that point forward, I was raised not only by my mother but by my maternal grandmother, my great-aunt, and our "adopted" great-grandmother—all who lived in the home. While my mother's marriages ended and there was no longer an everyday, ever-present father in the home, I was raised by amazing women—strong women, independent women ... opinionated, outspoken, and forthright women. Their home became our home, and I was blessed to be under their care and guidance.

While the move was needed and necessary for plenty of reasons, what I was left with was that the men in my mother's life, and consequently in mine, didn't last. They either walked away or the relationship ended for reasons that had nothing to do with me. I'm clear about that, but, of course, I didn't always know that. What stings the most is that bio dad walked away and didn't come back. He made a choice that excluded me from his life and he from mine. Forever. A weight that I've carried my entire life.

When the one man in your life, the one who is responsible for you being here—and who was supposed to be with you as you grew up, faced challenges, and learned needed lessons with his help and guidance—walks away, what does that mean? When he who was supposed to pick you up when you fell down and encourage you when you were discouraged, does not—what do you do? When he who would cause you to smile just because he walked into the room, who would hold you tight when you were afraid, tell you he'd never let anything bad happen to you, and that he would love you no matter what, isn't there—what do you do with that? When you wished he would have been there to tell you how brave you are, how smart you are, and believing him, you would try to be that every day. But he's not there—then what? When he walks away and never comes back ... you are left wondering if you ever even mattered. And when he has never been a part of your life, and seemingly never wanted to be ... you believe you couldn't have ever mattered.

But I'm Okay, Right?

My life seemingly started over at 11 years old with all of the typical trials and angst of a tween, then teenager, and into young adulthood. I was fortunate to have every opportunity my closest friends had. Well, mostly—the difference being, they all had their fathers. Fortunately, I never felt excluded or treated differently because I had an *absent* father. However, I did feel different at times. Their fathers were in their lives. Their fathers chose to be present and actively engaged. Their fathers knew every-thing about them, saw (or at least talked to) them every day. My friends had to answer to their fathers for their behavior, grades, activities, friends, chores, dating—all the things little girls and big girls have to talk to their daddies about. My friends had time with their fathers, they received words of wisdom, were walked through teachable moments, discussed lessons learned, and were showered with affection.

I had a stepfather I was still connected to—he was the only father I had ever known, and he was the biological father of my siblings. But he "fathered" us from very far away. We were on the east coast, and he was in California. Even though ... I was okay. I was loved, supported, and cared for by many. Most of my mom's family was in our hometown, and they were never too far away from us when needed. It takes a village, you know, and my mom had brought us to her village. And as I said, I was okay.

The Turning Point

Anderson explains that although abandonment begins with the loss of love and connection, it does not end there—it can surface as fear, unresolved grief, or patterns that quietly shape our relationships and hold us back from fully stepping into who we're becoming.[1]

I had moved through most of my life hoping I appeared to have it all together, to know exactly what I was doing—but I didn't have it all together, and I didn't know what I was doing. I'm not saying I lived a lie, I'm just saying there was safety in pretense—hiding what I didn't want the world to know about me. No one needed to know how terrified

---

1   Andersen, Susan. *The Journey From Abandonment to Healing*. Berkley Books, 2014.

I was of making mistakes, looking bad or foolish, getting it wrong, and being seen in a negative way. Why would I risk allowing anyone the ability to see all the reasons I could not be chosen, but was abandoned and left behind? I suffered many years with the wounds of abandonment and what many call a "father wound,"[2] and I didn't know it. I did not know that who I believed myself to be and how I functioned—my identity—had been impacted by this unhealed wound.

While I didn't know that I was *wounded*, my resulting perfectionism (didn't always know it was there or that there was a word for it) gave me something to strive for. I pursued a way of being that looked goal-driven and achievement-oriented with grace and ease. Surely this way of being would make me look good enough and would protect me from ... from what? From being abandoned again, disappointed, and heartbroken? Of course. But it also *protected* me from discovering who I was meant to be—my authentic, courageous self—and how to live a full life ... a life that I could choose to build and fill with joy and passion on my own terms.

Again, I needed answers and was driven by an overwhelming need to understand, so I turned to counseling. It was actually a suggestion by an administrator at my college who realized I was struggling with finances, study habits, time management, self-esteem, and figuring out who I would be on this path to being an educated adult (the realization was really from a near meltdown in her office).

---

2   Stephens, Kia. *Overcoming Father Wounds: Exchanging Your Pain for God's Perfect Love.* Revell, 2023.

The struggle was real because I had never found *just being* so hard. I couldn't understand why everything seemed so challenging and why I couldn't find my footing. I had been a really good student, I had friends, I dated, I enjoyed being a young person living my life to the fullest, right? No. It was all hard and confusing, challenging and daunting, and I didn't know what I was doing—I felt like I was lost in the dark and had no idea as to how I would find my way. So, I took the suggestion and made an appointment in the Student Counseling Center. I met with my very first counselor—and the light eventually came on.

This was the beginning of my healing. I no longer had to be in the darkness of not understanding bio dad's choice to walk away. I had support in a way that I had not before—I could ask questions of this objective, empathetic listener, and we could talk about whatever came up, explore possibilities, and bring clarity to what had been so challenging and disheartening. I now had the opportunity to better understand who I was then, who I wanted to be, and how I could get there in spite of bio dad's absence. I began to see that being abandoned and wounded was an experience I had endured, was not my fault, and did not have to define me. I could choose who I would be.

A Question-Guided Journey

My journey from abandonment to healing began in my early twenties. It didn't happen all at once—it unfolded over time. In quiet prayers, in pages filled with thoughts and sprinkled with tears, in moments of reflection, study, and honest conversations with counselors/therapists, friends, and spiritual coaches, I began to give voice to what I had carried for so long. Healing has come in layers, and even now, it continues.

What kept me moving forward were the questions I couldn't ignore—the ones that pushed me to understand the aforementioned "father wound." It's not always something you can see, but you can feel it. *The Attachment Project* describes it as the emotional and psychological pain, insecurity, and trauma that can grow from having a father who was absent, emotionally unavailable, neglectful, or abusive.[3] It begins in absence, but it doesn't stay there—it can shape how we see ourselves, how we love, and how we show up in the world.

The Questions I Couldn't Ignore

- *What do I do with the pain of abandonment and this "father wound"?*

- *How do I forgive the biological father I've never met and probably never will?*

- *How do I get free from carrying the emotional weight of a broken heart ... a heart broken by the man who was supposed to be my everything, teach me everything, protect me from everything, but chose to walk away instead?*

- *How do I finish this never-ending story of abandonment, hurt, and fear, and find a new beginning of hope, freedom, joy, and the kind of love that is aligned with God's plan for my life?*

---

3   "The Father Wound: What is It and How to Heal." *The Attachment Project*, attachmentproject.com/psychology/father-wound. Accessed March 2026.

I Had to Do the Work

I had to allow myself to feel the full range of feelings (i.e., curiosity, anger, grief, rejection, indifference, compassion, fear, etc.). But I didn't want to feel my feelings.

As a child, I was overcome by feelings, and it was very easy to cry—whether I was mad, scared, or upset about almost anything. It was like not knowing where the feelings belonged or how to truly express them ... so I would just cry. As an adult, I didn't want to feel my feelings because I didn't want to be overwhelmed by them—I needed to remain in control ... and I never could. Anger and fear would always get the best of me.

My anger reflected everything that I could not change, could not manage, and could not understand—no wonder it felt uncontrollable. Fear was the worst and also felt out of control—it often felt like terror with the need to run and hide. And who wants to feel that? With professional support, I came to know that my anger and fear stemmed from a lack of another feeling, a need that had not fully been met—emotional safety. This need, referenced in *Maslow's Hierarchy of Needs*, involves the need for trust, stability, freedom from fear, and supportive relationships.[4] As my healing progressed, being able to declare emotional safety for myself became my answered prayer.

I also had to allow myself to grieve for the father-daughter relationship that never was. I named the loss (everything I thought bio dad should have been for me, and everything that he was not), and allowed myself to feel the feelings

---

4   Pichère, Pierre, and Carly Probert. *Maslow's Hierarchy of Needs*. Namur, Belgium, 50Minutes.com, 17 Aug. 2015.

that came with the grief (sadness, anger, confusion, long-ing, and acceptance). And I prayed about it, journaled about it, and talked about it until I was able to release what never was.

I had to separate the story from my identity

I came to know that the abandonment did not have to define me. Whatever happened, how it happened, or even because it happened, had nothing to do with my worth, my value, or who I chose to be any day of my life. The mere fact that I don't know my bio dad, wouldn't know him if he knocked on my door, is unfortunate. It has impacted my life in various ways—but it does not mean that I am unwanted or that I am not worth knowing. My bio dad abandoning me has everything to do with his (in)capacity, circumstances, and/or choices. And nothing to do with who I am.

I had to accept that I may never get all the answers.

The one question that I've always had that may never be answered is if I mattered. Why didn't I matter to my biological father? A personal development course I took years ago asserted that we all have an "unanswerable" question. Through a facilitated exercise by a trained professional, I discovered that mine was "Do I matter?" Feeling the need to ask the question leads one to believe that an answer is required in order to agree or disagree. But the truth is that I do matter. Whether I ask the question or not, whether it's answered or not ... I matter. Further, it's not even a question to ask or be answered. God, as my Father, says I do.

Psalm 139:13-14 states: "For you created my inmost being; you knit me together in my mother's womb. I praise you because I am fearfully and wonderfully made; your works are wonderful; I know that full well" (NIV).

Not knowing what you think you should know can leave you feeling as though a part of you is unfinished or incomplete. I've felt that a chapter of my life had not been written, or at least it had not been made available to me. I wanted my life and who I was to make sense, but there was a piece, a parent—my father—missing.

My questions about my bio dad had to do with the puzzle of my origin and where I fit, and I wanted all the pieces. Instead, I would have to learn to live with unanswered questions and some ambiguity. But—I could decide that the missing pieces were only a part of my story—not the whole story, and not definitive. What I realized is that my life story didn't end with the missing chapter. God has written my story, and not all of the chapters are available to me. But I get to contribute and participate in all of them.

I had to bring closure on my own terms

Early in my journey to better understand myself and my relationships, a therapist encouraged me to seek closure with my bio dad. While it was extremely unlikely it could or would be face-to-face, I could write a letter (send it, burn it, tear it to shreds) where I could include what his absence has meant, what I needed from him, and/or any number of questions I may have had. I could engage in the "empty chair" technique used by therapists to assist clients in processing emotions and resolving internal conflicts by externalizing them and confronting them. And more importantly, I could say what I'm choosing for me because—although he didn't choose me by being in my life and the father I deserved—God chose me, my mom chose me, and I chose me. And that was enough.

I had to redefine what forgiveness means

There is no excuse for the wounding that abandonment can cause, but forgiveness provides a choice—to stop carrying the weight of it. Forgiveness is not about approval, nor pretending it is okay. It's about releasing the emotional burden of what was never meant to be held.

I can't name the exact moment forgiveness happened, but I know what made it possible: reclaiming the truth of who I am—loved, cared for, wanted, and chosen. In redefining forgiveness, I stopped seeing it as something that required bio dad's participation and began to understand it as something that restored me. It gave me back my energy, lifted up my sense of self, and freed me from waiting and accepting so little when I deserved so much more. From that place, I released my need for answers. I remain open to them, even curious but no longer dependent on them for my identity.

I had to recognize who I became without him

By God's grace, the love of my family, the support of good friends and mentors, and my willingness to do the work, I became who I am without him. Choosing myself allowed me to release the younger version of me who carried so many unanswered questions, who wondered why her biological father did not choose her, regardless. It meant letting go of the coping strategies that once protected me but began to limit me as I grew, and releasing the quiet terror that surfaced whenever I felt exposed or vulnerable.

I understand now that what happened shaped me, but it did not diminish or define me. And once I truly believed that, everything shifted. Feeling emotionally safe within allowed me to be seen and heard without fear—and to live my life more fully, on my own terms.

An Invitation from Me to You

Your early life may have begun with circumstances that you didn't choose—such as an absent father. Even when parts of your life are outside your control, you still get to choose what you do with the life that follows. Choosing yourself is not about fixing the past—it's about choosing what your story means now and choosing life consciously. My guiding questions were specific to what I needed to heal and to be free from the emotional weight of being abandoned by my biological father. They allowed me to choose myself and do the necessary, life-freeing work. Your guiding questions obviously don't have to mirror mine. However, I'd like to encourage you to consider the following:

- **Invest in knowing yourself** – Who are you beyond your roles (i.e., spouse, parent, provider, caretaker)? Self-knowledge is a huge form of freedom.

- **Face your wounds instead of ignoring them** – That's emotional courage; you do not have to carry old pain. Examine it, talk about it, and heal it. Self-care is self-love.

- **Exercise and maintain your agency** – The choices remain your own (i.e., education, career, hobbies, travel, etc.). Your freedom allows you to explore, grow, and build experiences that matter to you.

- **Explore and discover your purpose** – Doing so allows you to embrace who you are and who you want, or are meant, to be.

- **Choose you** – Let go of trying to prove yourself, earn approval, or measure up to some expectation. Getting to know yourself, accept yourself, and forgive yourself, if need be, is not only a form of freedom but loving yourself as well.

And when you do choose yourself, you begin to shift how you see your life. What once felt like proof of abandonment, or not being chosen or wanted, starts to be reexamined, reinterpreted. As you recognize God's love, grace, and mercy woven through your story—in every moment of joy, every embrace, every sunrise and sunset, and in the people who showed up and stood by you—you begin to gather new evidence. Evidence that challenges the wound. Evidence that tells a fuller truth. And over time, your identity reorganizes. You realize your life isn't about being abandoned or wounded. It's about being chosen. It's about being loved. And the truth is—you always were.

> Therefore, as God's chosen people, holy and dearly loved, clothe yourselves with compassion, kindness, humility, gentleness and patience. (Colossians 3:12, NIV)

Unimaginable: Finding God's Faithfulness During Financial Hardship or Life Transitions

By Stacey Gawthrop

We had a routine. Life was moving in a familiar rhythm. Steve had worked for 14 years in a warehouse. With two sons and one on the way, our normal was being transformed from everything close by to flying over 500 miles to possibilities we could not yet see. God rarely announces his greatest works with clarity.

His design is often hidden ... but never uncertain.

Creation itself whispers this truth.

A caterpillar lives low to the ground, moving slowly, focused only on what is right in front of it—gathering what it needs for the day. Then, at the appointed time, it is drawn upward. It forms a cocoon, a place that, from the outside, looks like an ending.

But God has already written a different story.

Deep within the caterpillar's DNA are cells called imaginal cells—God-designed, dormant, waiting. And inside the stillness of the chrysalis, those cells awaken. What once was begins to dissolve, making way for something entirely new.

What looks like stillness ... what feels like the end ... is actually the beginning of something quietly unfolding.

This is not a fight for survival ... It is a surrender to transformation.

And in God's perfect timing, the unimaginable begins to unfold.

Just like that hidden work within the chrysalis, my husband and I, too, were being carried through a season we didn't fully understand—yet one that was quietly unfolding something new within us.

After years of waiting, everything finally seemed to be falling into place. Each detail fit together like pieces of a puzzle we had patiently worked on for so long.

For nearly ten years, my husband had been pursuing a life change—from working in a warehouse to stepping into a completely different calling as a Physician Assistant. Step by step, he completed every prerequisite, faithfully pressing through the process. Year after year, he applied, and each time he wasn't accepted meant another long year of waiting before he could try again. Now, for the fourth time, he had applied to the Physician Assistant program in Pomona, California.

But as we stood on the threshold of possibility, a quiet question settled in our hearts—*where is God pointing us, and will we trust Him enough to follow?*

The Finger of God Will Never Point Where the Hand of God Cannot Provide

I was eight months pregnant with our third son, and even his timing seemed heaven-sent. Our son would be six weeks old when the program began—just enough time for us to settle into a rhythm before this new chapter started.

We had just purchased a home close to the college. My part-time job was nearby, steady, and sufficient to carry us through. My dear friends were ready to come alongside me and help me begin homeschooling our kindergartener. Our families lived close by. Our church community surrounded us with support, love, and familiarity.

It wasn't just that things were falling into place—it was how beautifully they were doing so. It felt like blessing upon blessing, confirmation upon confirmation.

God was so good.

Deep down, I didn't wonder *if* he would get in this time—I was certain of it. My faith felt steady, confident, secure. I even had a phrase that I had heard on the radio that I would say often, a quiet declaration I carried in my heart:

The finger of God will never point where the hand of God cannot provide.

And I believed it.

The day before Steve's birthday—June 3—we stood outside in the front yard of our newly purchased home, talking with a few neighbors who had come by to welcome us. The evening stretched on longer than we expected, the kind of conversation that feels easy and full, as the sun slowly dipped below the horizon. We watched it set right there from our front yard, unaware that something important was already waiting for us inside.

At some point while we were out there, the phone must have rung. We didn't hear it.

It wasn't until we walked back into the house that I noticed the blinking red light on our answering machine. We looked at each other, curious, and then pressed the button together.

"Hi, this message is for Steve. This is the PA program in Pomona. I have some news I'd like to share with you—if you can give me a call back tomorrow morning by 8:00 a.m."

We both froze for a second, then looked at each other with growing excitement.

"Steve ... I think you got in the program!"

There was something almost sweet about the timing— because we had been outside, he couldn't return the call right away. He would have to wait until morning ... his birthday morning.

That night, sleep came in short stretches. Our minds were full, our hearts even more so. Early the next day, we drove to my mom's house so she could watch the kids while Steve made the call.

I stood close enough to hear his side of the conversation, watching every expression on his face.

"Steve?"

"Yes, this is him," I heard Steve say.

"Well, I want to say congratulations to you, Steve. But I have some good news ... and maybe some difficult news."

My heart started pounding watching every expression he made.

"Okay ... go ahead," he said.

"Well, congratulations because you've been accepted into the PA program!"

"That's great!"

I couldn't contain myself—I started quietly jumping up and down, joy bubbling over as I watched him. This was it. This was what we had been praying for.

But then ... his expression shifted. His face grew serious. Then more serious.

"Yes... that is a big decision," he said slowly.

"Okay ... I understand. I'll be in touch by tomorrow morning."

He hung up.

"What happened?" I asked, my excitement now mixed with confusion.

He took a breath and explained. He *had* been accepted—but not to Pomona, where we had carefully built our plans. Instead, he was offered a spot in a satellite program this school had recently started in Chico, California.

"What? Where's that?" I said, my baby kicking in my tummy.

We pulled out an old map from my mom's end table and spread it open. Starting in Southern California, we traced our fingers upward ... and upward ... following the coastline nearly to Oregon. There it was—Chico. Over 500 miles from everything we had just set in place.

He had 24 hours to decide.

He was still number one on the waiting list for Pomona—the place we had planned our life around. But we were told that once people are accepted, they rarely turn it down. A spot there was unlikely to open.

Yet here he was—already accepted into Chico.

A door had opened ... just not the one we expected.

That day—Steve's birthday—I knew this opportunity was a gift, something he had prayed for and persevered toward for ten long years.

But it didn't look the way we thought it would.

We called our pastor, asking for wisdom. His advice was simple, yet not easy:

"Don't make a pro and con list—that will only quench what the Holy Spirit might be doing. Rather, each of you go into a separate room and ask God, 'Is this what You are inviting us into?'"

Steve didn't even need to go into another room. He already knew his answer.

I wasn't there yet.

At eight months pregnant, the weight of it all felt overwhelming. Leaving everything behind? The home we had just bought? Our families? Our friends? Our church? The support system we had carefully built?

How would we provide for our family of five? We had used nearly all of our savings to purchase our home, and now I would have to leave my job, leaving us without any income. The student loans would help, but they were meant to support a student, not an entire family.

Where would we even live?

What about homeschooling?

Who would help me now?

All the questions came rushing in at once.

I had faith that God would get him into the program—and He did.

But now, the question felt deeper.

Stacey ... do you trust Me with your whole life?

My own words echoed back to me: The finger of God will never point where the hand of God cannot provide. But now ... that belief was being tested. Because God was gently showing me something I hadn't fully understood before: Hope is open hands—surrendered to Him and His perfect plans.

But expectations? They are closed fists.

Clinging tightly to what we think should happen ... and when it doesn't, disappointment settles in, and we quietly begin to believe that somehow God has failed us.

And in that moment, I realized—He wasn't asking me to have it all figured out. He was asking me to open up my hands and let go and trust Him anyway.

The journey was only two years ... but it felt like everything.

Though it was the hardest decision I had ever faced, there was a quiet clarity beneath it all—no more waiting, no more wondering. The door we had been praying would open for ten years was finally open. All that remained was our yes.

I walked over to my husband, looked into his eyes, and with a steady, surrendered heart, I said,

"I choose yes. Happy birthday."

Those two years unfolded in ways we never could have planned. They were full—full of laughter, long days, shared meals, and the kind of friendships that seem to form almost overnight when you're all walking through the same stretching season. Our boys found fast friends in another family whose children matched ours in both age and energy, filling our days with noise and life. And then there was a 50-year-old student, without any family, named Frank—quiet, often alone—who slowly became part of our rhythm. Holidays at our table, simple evenings of conversation ... what began as an invitation became something much deeper.

Somehow, in the middle of being the ones in need, we found ourselves giving, too. A Bible placed into the hands of a young man searching for truth. Meals shared. Time given. We lived as best we could with open hands, trusting that God was weaving something meaningful through it all.

As graduation drew closer, everything began to pick up speed.

Interviews with classmates filled the calendar. Conversations shifted toward "what's next." One by one, our peers began walking into those final classes carrying good news. A job offer here. A signed contract there. Each announcement was met with cheers, applause, and celebration. We joined in wholeheartedly, clapping and smiling, certain it was only a matter of time before we would have our own news to share.

We had a place in mind—the rural health clinic where Steve had completed a rotation and his preceptorship in Family Practice. It felt right in every way. Familiar. Purposeful. And with the federal loan repayment program for PAs who work in rural areas, it would take care of the $75,000 in school debt we carried. It seemed like the kind of provision only God could orchestrate.

We kept praying the words that had carried us this far:

The finger of God will never point where the hand of God cannot provide.

The days moved quickly after that. We helped friends pack up their homes, loading boxes into cars filled with excitement and new beginnings. We celebrated milestones. We stood proudly as Steve walked across the stage and graduated—ten years of perseverance wrapped up in a single moment.

And then, just like that, the celebrations quieted. The house grew still. We found ourselves sitting on the couch one evening, our three boys playing on the rug in front of us, their laughter filling the room in that familiar, comforting way.

And it was in that ordinary, almost peaceful moment, that things suddenly became clear. Our family was the only one still waiting.

There's a strange kind of quiet that comes when you think you've reached the finish line ... only to realize there isn't one. There were no ribbons to break, no crowd cheering us on, and no one waiting to hand us our next steps. Just ... stillness.

It felt like running a long, exhausting race—one that had taken years of endurance, sacrifice, and unwavering focus—only to slow down at the end and find nothing there but an empty track stretching out ahead.

What do you do with that?

We had always imagined this moment differently. Graduation wasn't supposed to feel like a pause—it was supposed to feel like a launch. We thought a job would come quickly, almost naturally, like the next step in a well-ordered plan.

But one by one, his classmates had already packed up and moved on. New cities. New jobs. New beginnings. Their lives were already in motion.

And we were still ... here. There were no interviews. We did not have any clear direction. We were just waiting.

There's a rhythm to life when you're moving toward something. You wake up with purpose, with a list, with a sense of where your energy should go. Even in the busyness, there's comfort in knowing what the day holds. But then suddenly ... the calendar is blank.

Morning comes ... and instead of stepping into something certain, you find yourself standing in the quiet, unsure of where to place your next step. It wasn't loud. It wasn't dramatic. Just a quiet uncertainty settling in where confidence used to be.

Two of our boys were old enough to play soccer, so we signed them up. Before long, their practices and games became something we looked forward to—a rhythm in our days, a place to show up, to cheer, to feel a sense of movement again.

One afternoon, as Steve stood on the sidelines watching Jeremiah practice, the coach walked over and asked if he'd be willing to be his assistant coach.

Steve paused for a moment, thinking of his wide-open calendar, then smiled and said, "Sure ... why not?" He was there anyway.

The very next day, while watching Zach at his practice, another coach called out, asking if anyone could lend a hand. Without hesitation this time, Steve stepped forward again. And just like that, something small began to shift.

This was new for him. For years, his schedule had been too full—too structured—to step into moments like these. He had always been present, but now ... he was available.

And in that unexpected space, he found himself not just watching from the sidelines but stepping in.

I, on the other hand, was watching from the sidelines ... and I can't say I was quite as content. As I sat there, I watched my husband joyfully running up and down the field with a swarm of little boys chasing the soccer ball like bees around a honey pot. It was a sweet scene, one that should have made me smile fully, but instead, it stirred something deeper in me: the ache of waiting and the uncertainty of what was still to come.

What looked like a simple season on the sidelines was actually the beginning of something deeper that I couldn't yet see. God wasn't just filling our time ... He was reshaping my heart.

Open hands receive what clenched fists never could

But even as that truth began to settle in me, our circumstances remained unchanged. With each passing month, hope and uncertainty walked side by side.

The months after graduation came and went—June, then July, then August, and September quietly followed. Each new month carried the same quiet expectation: maybe this would be the time a job came through, a door opened, or something finally began to move.

But as the weeks passed, an unspoken question began to settle in ...

What if a job doesn't come?

Our savings were nearly gone. We had about $2,000 left on our only credit card—and that was it. And yet, somehow, even in the uncertainty, God kept meeting us. Not always in the ways we expected—but always in the ways we needed.

A longtime friend of Steve's from Southern California came to visit. Just having him there felt like a breath of fresh air—laughter, familiarity, the comfort of being known. After he left, we noticed a card sitting on the counter.

Inside was a simple note:

"Remember—the finger of God will never point where the hand of God cannot provide."

Tucked inside was $325.

Another dear friend took us out to dinner—blessing our whole family with a meal we didn't have to think twice about—and quietly left a card with $100 inside.

And one day, when groceries were running low, a box from our church showed up on our front porch. Shampoo, spaghetti, tomato sauce, bread ... simple things, but to us, they felt like abundance. Our boys were thrilled, pulling everything out one by one like it was a treasure. God was providing!

Then November came. And with it ... an interview! It had been months—so this felt big.

The position was in Watsonville, near Santa Cruz. Beautiful, coastal ... but far. It would mean starting over again in so many ways. Still, it was the only opportunity that had come since graduation, so we had high expectations.

We drove there together early on a Saturday morning, the sun shining as if to match our emotions. I dropped Steve off at the clinic and found a nearby fast-food restaurant to wait, passing the time and quietly praying.

At two o'clock, I pulled up in front of the small, quaint clinic to pick him up. He got into the driver's seat, and I quickly moved over, eager to hear everything.

"It went well," he said, smiling. He paused.

I leaned in. "What happened?"

He explained that they needed someone to work weekends, which wasn't a problem. But then came the part that changed everything. He would need to be fluent in Spanish, often working alone with a primarily Hispanic migrant population, which he was not.

As he spoke, I felt it ... that quiet sinking inside. This wasn't the outcome I had expected. I had pictured a celebration, a sense of relief. The moment we would finally say, *"This is it."* But it wasn't this time.

The drive home was long—three and a half hours—and heavy. We pulled onto the freeway in silence, both of us carrying the weight of another "not yet."

And then, about twenty minutes into the drive ... the van began to sputter.

Chug.

Chug.

Chug.

Steve carefully guided it to the side of the freeway just as the transmission gave out completely. And in that moment, it felt like everything in me sank.

Really, Lord? Even this?

Soon, we found ourselves in a tow truck, heading back to the nearest town. I had to make a phone call to my friend who was watching our sons to let her know we would not be coming home that night. We checked into a small hotel, waiting for AAA to tow us all the way back to Chico the next day. Steve made one more quick call to our mechanic to get an appointment set up.

And the repair cost? He said it would be $1,982. Almost exactly what we had left on our credit card.

Lying there in that quiet hotel room, I sensed the Lord gently speaking to my heart.

Do you see it now, Stacey?

You can't make anything happen.

I am the One in control.

His voice was not harsh, not condemning. It was steady and full of loving truth.

You don't have to figure everything out.

Put your hope in Me—not in the job, not in your plans, not in what you thought this would look like.

And somewhere along that long drive home the next day, I felt it—a shift I couldn't ignore. Something in me softened. A release from trying to work it out.

I had been holding so tightly to what I believed should happen ... gripping my expectations with closed fists. But slowly, almost without realizing it, my hands began to open.

Palms up.

Surrendered.

Trusting.

And in that quiet surrender, I began to understand something I hadn't seen before—

Open hands receive what clenched fists never could.

"God," I whispered in the quiet of my heart,

"I refuse to focus on what I lack and instead focus my eyes on your fullness. I refuse to let worry lead me any longer, and instead I release the grip I've had on how I thought things should unfold—the conversations, the timing, the answers I was expecting. I see now that I cannot hold Your peace while my hands are clenched around my own expectations.

"So today, I let go.

"I open my hands in hope to You—fully surrendered to Your provision, Your timing, and Your ways. Even when I don't understand, I choose to trust that You are leading me through this season with purpose and love.

"Quiet my worries, Lord. Steady my heart. Teach me to hope in You. I believe ... truly believe ... that You are able to do immeasurably more than I could ever ask or imagine.

"In Jesus name, amen."

I made a quiet decision in that moment—

And as I let go, His peace came in with renewed hope. Not all at once, but gently, steadily filling the spaces fear had occupied. It changed the way I saw everything. Not our circumstances, but *Him.* I began to trust His ability, His faithfulness. I believed in His unseen hand orchestrating a story far greater than I could understand.

I wrote this poem in my journal the next day:

Expectation calls it death.

> Hope watches for resurrection.

Expectation says, *nothing is happening.*

> Hope knows that *God is still moving.*

Expectation sees the caterpillar

> and believes the story ends in the dust—

Hope waits, knowing wings

> are being formed in hidden places.

Expectation stands in the ruins and says, "It's over."

> Hope kneels in the same place
> and whispers, not yet.

Expectation sees empty hands,
closed doors, unanswered prayers—

> Hope lifts open palms
> and makes room for the unimaginable.

What feels hidden and uncertain is often God unfolding something unimaginable

Walking into our home the next day, there was a message waiting for us from a friend asking if Steve could meet him for coffee the next morning at his office.

He had no idea what had just happened.

But God did.

The next morning, Steve came into our bedroom, holding something in his hand. His voice was quiet but full.

"He gave me a check," he said. "He said we don't have to pay it back."

Earlier that morning, I had gone over our bills—rent, electricity, the basics for December. I knew exactly what we needed ... down to the dollar.

As I looked at the check, I felt something rise in me that I hadn't felt in a while. Not just relief ... but awe. It was enough. The check amount was enough to cover every bill and even a little extra for groceries and gas.

God hadn't just provided. He had *seen us.* And somehow, deep down, I knew—this was only the beginning.

It was three weeks now before Christmas, and we had no money to even think about buying our three sons Christmas presents, let alone any other extended family gifts. We were thankful our rent and utilities were paid for!! And we ended up using the $400 that was meant for a suit for interviews to buy groceries instead. But we were hopeful.

My friend called and asked if their home study group could come over the following week. I was a little curious why, but she simply said they wanted to encourage us and pray with us—if we were open to it.

The night came when the group—about six people—gathered in our small family room. Wanting to make it special, we had prepared a few desserts, and we spent the beginning of the evening simply enjoying them together.

Our son Jeremiah, who was seven at the time, asked if he could play a song on his violin. We smiled and said yes, and as he played, the room grew quiet in the sweetest way.

When he finished, the group leader gently spoke up and smiled. He shared how they had come that evening with the hope of being a blessing to us—instead, they were being blessed.

Then he reached into his bag and pulled out a thick envelope, handing it to me. He encouraged me to open it. Inside was a beautiful card—and tucked within it were gift cards ... more than I had ever seen at one time. Gift cards for groceries, for gas, even for a toy store for the boys.

For a moment, I couldn't even speak. We just sat there, completely overwhelmed by the kindness, the generosity, and the unmistakable provision of God. But that wasn't all.

Before they left, they shared that they had mentioned our situation to others in the church and gently said, "Don't be surprised if you see a few more gifts coming your way."

We smiled, not quite knowing what to expect. But over the next week ... it began. One by one, people showed up at our door.

A pair of roller blades.

Bags of groceries.

A hockey game.

A basketball hoop for the driveway.

Three bicycles.

And then more ... so many thoughtful gifts that it became hard to keep track of them all.

Each knock at the door felt like another reminder—

We were seen, we were loved, and we were being cared for in ways we never could have arranged ourselves.

Our boys were overjoyed. Their excitement filled the house with laughter and wonder, turning what could have been a season of lack into one of abundance.

And for me, there was a quiet joy too. With the gift cards, I was able to go out and choose gifts of my own—small things, but meaningful—so that I could give to our boys from my heart as well.

In a season where I had felt so empty-handed ... God gently placed something back into my hands to give.

We were experiencing more than we could have ever imagined, our hearts full as we said, "God, this is more than enough ... truly more than enough." But God wasn't finished.

Out of nowhere, Steve received a call from the rural health clinic where he had done his preceptorship—the very place we had once hoped and prayed he might work, even when there had been no opening.

He quietly stepped into the kitchen to take the call.

And in that moment, I felt it—a familiar stirring. A memory rushed back from two years earlier, when he had stood in a kitchen, on our phone, receiving the news that he had been accepted into the PA program. I found myself watching him again, wondering ... *what is happening this time?*

Then I saw it ... that smile. The kind that says everything before a single word is spoken.

He walked back toward me and said, "Guess what? That was Heather from the health center ... she asked if I could come to work on Monday."

I could hardly take it in.

The week before Christmas—December 19—when most people are slowing down, taking time off, and stepping away from work, my husband was being invited in.

It felt like the most unimaginable gift ever! And he didn't even need a suit for an interview. But God still wasn't finished.

Soon after, the director called him into her office and told him she would personally go to bat for him to have his school loans repaid.

Within six months or so, we received the news—he had been accepted into the federal loan repayment program.

Every single dollar of our $75,000 in debt would be paid off in just three years of employment! At the very clinic he had hoped for. The very place God had quietly held for him all along.

We stood there in awe. The words that had carried us through every question, every delay, every moment of uncertainty came rushing back to my heart—

The finger of God will never point where the hand of God cannot provide.

And here it was ... right in front of us. It was proven, tried, and true.

It's in the hardest times that the unimaginable happens.

We never imagined that God would do all He did when we were in the middle of it. We had done all we could do, but God hadn't even begun to do what He wanted. When I let go, it gave God room to work in our lives.

God had done far more than we could have ever imagined.

And in that moment, it was undeniable—

His plans had never been delayed.

They had been unfolding ...

What looked like nothing was happening

was actually God unfolding something unimaginable.

ACTION ITEMS

Your story may not be unfolding the way you would have chosen it to go. And although everything around you looks like nothing is happening and it's hard to believe anything *good,* let alone *great,* is around the corner, you can trust God with your future because he is already there!

1. Write these scriptures on a slip of paper or any scripture that God shows you, and fold the paper and put it in your pocket. Hold onto these promises, reading them throughout the day when you are tempted to doubt God's work in your lives.

   "Now to Him who is able to do immeasurably
   more than all we ask or imagine, according
   to His power that is at work within us."
   —*Ephesians 3:20, NIV*

"And my God will supply every need of yours according to his riches in glory in Christ Jesus."

—*Philippians 4:19, ESV*

"'For I know the plans I have for you,' declares the LORD, 'plans to prosper you and not to harm you, plans to give you hope and a future.'"

—*Jeremiah 29:11, NIV*

Or write them on a sticky note and put it on your bathroom mirror, so you see it first thing in the morning.

2. Pray the prayer in the story:

Dear God—

I choose to turn my focus away from what I lack and fix my eyes on Your fullness. I will no longer let worry lead me, and I release the need to control how things unfold—the conversations, the timing, the outcome I had hoped for. I've come to see that I cannot hold onto peace while my hands are tightly gripping what I want to happen.

I open my hands up to you, Lord, surrendered to your provision, your timing, your ways of taking me through this season.

Quiet my worries, Lord. Steady my heart. Teach me to hope in You.

I believe ... truly believe ... that You are able to do immeasurably more than I could ever ask or imagine.

In Jesus name, amen.

Write down in your journal anything the Lord is showing you to release. Listen for his truth about your worries and declare His promises over your situation.

Chapter 4

The Night I Let Go: Trusting the Lord in the Midst of the Storm

By Katherine Freeman

It was an eerie summer night, and the air felt heavy under dark, low-hanging clouds. I shivered as I ran out of the car to my son's apartment door. I knocked, but there was no answer. I knocked again, but there was no answer. *It had taken me what, 30 minutes to drive here? Surely David's okay ... surely.* I knocked again. No answer. He had said just 30 minutes ago that he could not go on like this any longer ... that he was going to kill himself.

He had threatened suicide many times, and I had always come running, but something about tonight felt dire—I was overcome with dread and fear. I wanted David to come out of his apartment now. I stepped back up to the door—I knocked again. No answer. I prayed, "Dear God, please let him be alright."

I walked back to my car and sat behind the wheel. Maybe he had gone out somewhere, and here I was worrying and frantic over nothing. I called 911 and asked if they could perform a wellness check on my son. I gave them the reason and the address. "Lord, please, please let everything be alright, I promise I'll do anything you want me to do in this life if you'll spare David's life. Please touch him, Lord, please let him know you are there."

I had prayed something like this for the last five years since his diagnosis of schizophrenia. I had tried to make his life worth living—giving him a home of his own, bringing him food, taking him out to dinner, meeting him for walks, and going on shopping trips. It wasn't enough ... never enough. He would call, wanting more, wanting something I couldn't give him—relief from the voices and peace in his heart.

I was searching for an answer to a problem that only God could solve. When he was first diagnosed, I thought that bringing David home would help him to cope with the illness. But it ended in sleepless nights. The voices in his head kept him awake; he'd slam doors, shocking myself and my husband out of a sound sleep. He would then go outside to yell at the voices to shut up; he was so loud I thought the neighbors would call.

My daughter took him to live with her in the Pacific Northwest, which actually worked well for a while. David thrived. Then he lost his job, and his behavior became erratic again. The psychiatrist was very kind when I traveled there to assess the situation. He said, "Sometimes the illness trumps the meds—even when the patient is totally compliant." When we found out that David was spending the nights riding around on public transit, unsuspectingly giving away his cell phone by allowing someone to "borrow" it.

We decided to act and had him committed. But involuntary commitment just meant that he would stay in a mental hospital for a longer period of time, sleeping almost constantly. On one visit, I remember sitting with him while he slept, tossing and turning, gasping for air. When I sat with him in the day room, he and everyone there were in a medicated stupor. I knew that staying there was not an improvement to his life; it was no kind of life. I worked to have him released. When I brought him back home, I thought nutrition, supplements, and exercise would be the answer—but David resisted all suggestions. He insisted on taking care of his food, medications, and exercise routines (or lack thereof) himself. He eventually was able to move out of the house.

Living alone was difficult for him. I would bring groceries, give him money for meals, transportation, and household needs. He ended up in mental hospitals dozens of times a year. I was physically, emotionally, and financially drained.

There are a number of things that began to play on my mind when my previously bright, cheerful child was diagnosed with a mental illness. First, I began to question everything about his childhood and my parenting. I thought that I should have presented more bible teachings when he was young, that I should have focused more on his well-being. I wondered if he had stayed in his hometown high school instead of going to a gifted school, if he would have been more stable. I started to question my own sanity. I questioned every choice I ever made; I tried to recruit the whole family into solving this problem. I thought that I had disappointed God in the way I raised my children, and I had doubted God's favor.

I would go without sleep, I would read about other parent's journeys with their children with a similar diagnosis. Educating myself helped me to understand David, but it didn't edify me; it didn't give me much hope because the world doesn't really have much to offer a person with a mental diagnosis. Doctors prescribe medication and therapy, but there isn't a good prognosis. I grieved the loss of the son I once had.

Then there was the night that I panicked after he threatened suicide and stood outside his apartment, praying that God would spare his life and David would turn to Him. Two officers arrived; I followed them to the door, and they knocked. Much to my amazement, the door opened. David stood there in a turquoise towel, light shining on his dripping hair. "I was in the shower," he said, looking past them at me.

The officers questioned him. After a while, as soon as he denied being suicidal, the officers left. We stood there for a moment in the doorway. I asked, "Do you want to go for groceries?" "Yeah," he said. "I'll get dressed." Then he closed the door.

Back in my car, I shook—relieved, emptied. I felt God's gentle hand steadying me. It was clear to me then, through the Lord's gentle presence, that God was truly the one taking care of David. I knew within my heart of hearts that I could not rescue him anymore. The Lord was guiding me to place him on the altar and trust God with what I could not control.

A lightness came into my heart as David sheepishly sat next to me and we pulled out of the parking lot into the light of the streetlamp.

> "You will show me the path of life; In Your presence is fullness of joy; at Your right hand are pleasures forevermore."
>
> *—Psalm 16:11, NKJV*

Spiritual Renewal

After that night, when I realized that all my worry wasn't helping anything, and all my striving wasn't going to make him better, my relationship with the Lord Jesus became central, and I started to pursue a stronger prayer life. I started to pray as a beloved child of the Most High God. I realized that I was loved with an eternal love. I accepted God's love for me. I had always thought that my worth was measured by how much I could accomplish and how well

I performed. I realized that the position I was in as David's mother had a purpose in my becoming more like Christ. Instead of begging God for release from the situation, I started to pray for God's will in David's life, for God to bless him and help him; I began to sit in God's presence and relate to Jesus as my friend, my helper, my savior, my counselor. Through this practice of His presence, He gave and still gives me deep abiding peace.

I took a Bible study course about the Psalms with women at church; being with other women who were struggling with their children's problems helped me to realize that I was not alone in my circumstances. The bible study itself, "Discovering God in the Psalms," which I ended up completing on my own, was a blessing at every turn; I realized through the study that God was still reaching out to me.

I took a course at church that was taught through the training of The Ultimate Journey at Christ-Life Ministries. The course helped me to realize that I was holding onto old hurts and walking around like a wounded child. Through this course, I was able to heal from my own trauma and come to a place of ministering to others. I realized that I did not have to do it all! There have been days when I just couldn't make it to help David when he wanted me to; he later told me that someone else helped him. I was so relieved and knew that God cared about him more than I did; that God would continue to help him when I was no longer able to. I learned that I did not have to live without joy to make David's life better; I had to seek what God wanted me to accomplish in this life, and do it.

My Action Items

I started to look for some avenues to regain my own life and a sense of well-being: I knew that I had to be strong myself in order to help my child.

A counselor showed me that I could live my life without taking on everyone else's problems.

Learning to quilt gave a new lease on life. I found great joy in making quilts for family and friends. A hobby is such a great way to connect with people who enjoy similar activities. I'm still excited about my next project!

I joined a research study that required daily exercise; that gave me the physical boost I needed to stay active.

By refusing to allow my thoughts about my son to take up all my time, I started to pay more attention to my other children and my husband. I continue to try to strengthen the bonds between myself and other family members.

> "And the peace of God, which surpasses all understanding, will guard your hearts and minds through Christ Jesus."
> —*Philippians 4:7, NKJV*

God has given me that peace that surpasses all understanding; David is still battling his demons, and I continue to believe that one day, God will heal him. I help him as often as I can, but I do so without struggling; I love and accept him as he is, and I just express my love for him in my caring for him. I have faith that God has a timing and a purpose. As children of God, we are to become like the servant Christ is, trusting him to provide what we need when we care for our loved ones. There are NO limitations in Christ; He is limitless. As we obey Him and His voice, we will find that peace that is beyond understanding.

Next Steps

- If you, dear reader, are a caregiver, parent, sister, brother, aunt, or uncle of a person with schizophrenia or other serious mental illness, I would suggest the following:

- Seek the Lord with all of your heart, mind, soul, and strength, read about Him, and spend time with Him in prayer and meditation. Read the word of God and wait to hear His still small voice.

- Seek prayer and help with any self-healing you need.

- Find time to do things you enjoy, even if they are just short, momentary times in your day that you can fill with a hobby, sport, or favorite activity.

- Find people who understand you and are willing to listen to you.

- Trust the Lord with your loved one; He cares for them, too.

Renewal by Fire: A Journey of Hope, Healing, and Transformation

By Lindsay Koach

"LORD, BY SUCH THINGS PEOPLE LIVE; AND MY SPIRIT FINDS LIFE IN THEM TOO. YOU RESTORED ME TO HEALTH AND LET ME LIVE. SURELY IT WAS FOR MY BENEFIT THAT I SUFFERED SUCH ANGUISH. IN YOUR LOVE YOU KEPT ME FROM THE PIT OF DESTRUCTION; YOU HAVE PUT ALL MY SINS BEHIND YOUR BACK."
—ISAIAH 38:16-17, NIV

It was October of 2014. I had just left the endocrinologist's office after discussing blood work results with my doctor. Severe afternoon fatigue, low body temperature, brain fog, sugar cravings, and poor sleep had been intensifying over several months. I'll never forget sitting in my car in the parking lot after the appointment. Watching the rain hit my windshield, tears were flooding my eyes and falling down my cheeks just like the water droplets racing down the glass. A myriad of thoughts, confusion, and then feeling the pit in my stomach. *How was this happening?*

I thought I was a healthy person. As a newer mom, I didn't have time to deal with this. I wanted more answers, and I wanted to fix everything as quickly as possible. My desire for the answers and wanting to "fix things" came from a lifelong need to feel in control. This had been with me since I was a child, when I had to create solutions and find security on my own. I struggled with trust issues and wanted to do everything myself. Facing various times in my life when I felt unsupported or disappointed in those closest to me, I took most things in stride and handled them on my own. As much as I clung to that coping mechanism, it was something that I would have to let go of in order to heal.

The endocrinologist's words didn't sit well with me. I felt that there had to be a better explanation, as well as a better plan. "You're just genetically inclined to have hypothyroidism. Many women are, and it's at a hormonal shift, like pregnancy or during perimenopause, when it starts. It's common. You'll have to take medication to regulate it. We'll also need to do a hormone panel to see what's happening with your estrogen levels."

Medicating wasn't a path I wanted to take. I wanted to know *why* this was happening and how I could fix it. My mind went back to 2008 when my dear friend took me to a cooking class at the home of a local Holistic Health Counselor named Janet. I had been experiencing irritable bowel syndrome and migraines for quite some time, and after sharing this with my friend, she explained that making nutritional changes may be the key. My friend then shared how much that had been helping her with her arthritis symptoms. I went with her for a Saturday cooking workshop, and this was the official start to understanding the medicinal power of food. I implemented what we learned, and pretty soon my digestion leveled out, and the headaches stopped.

Fast forward six years. Life had changed quite a bit. I had a one-year-old at home, a busy husband in the thick of fielding demands of a growing business, and I had been spending a lot of time alone with my baby boy. Being a new mom is a beautiful experience, but as every mom knows, it has its challenges. The biggest hurdle for me was taking care of myself, but I was comforted by the large cultural acceptance of this flaw. Moms like myself were sharing slices of their experiences on social media or on the playground. The typical gamut was shared between all of us living on little sleep, scraping up whatever food we could eat, and, of course, depending on caffeine.

There was also a sense of feeling alone in my role as a new mom due to not being able to lean on my own mother in ways that I had hoped for. Unfortunately, she has unresolved trauma and gaps in her own sense of feeling loved and supported due to her childhood and the circumstances surrounding having a mother who battled alcoholism. I have always done my best to lead with love and be understanding of her struggles, but it's difficult to handle at times, especially when you become a mother yourself.

I had settled into unhealthy habits that I knew were emotionally driven, and I lost my bearings from what I learned from the Holistic Health Counselor I had seen years ago. As I sat in the car fumbling for tissues, I pulled out my phone and called her number. Once we set a time to meet, a lot of the uneasiness melted away. I felt that sense of control again that I was always trying to maintain. The familiar quest for control would stick with me for a while, but the surrender eventually came, and thank God it did.

The Lessons of Trusting and Surrendering

The two-year journey that I'm sharing in this chapter brought me to a level of clarity and empowerment that only God can provide. Through this journey, I learned to trust the Lord when He places a mountain in my path. The intention of the challenges God places before us is not to punish us or throw us off, but to renew us and develop a deeper relationship with Him. If I had not experienced the journey with my thyroid and hormonal depletion, I would not be who I am today. I would not have discovered the promises kept when choosing to be obedient to the Lord, or experienced the paradigm shift that changed my understanding of health and wellbeing, which ultimately shifted the trajectory of my entire life. My family grew as a result of this journey, and only God can do that. Only He can lead us and provide everyone and everything we need. At the time, I felt like I was being led on a wild goose chase. Looking back, I am thankful I trusted the process, with all its twists and turns, because it gave me new life. It gave me hope.

Lesson #1 Re-Commitment: The Renewing of My Relationship with the Lord

The beginning of this journey led me to commit my repeated offense of not trusting someone or something. In this case, it would be both. I had a meeting with Janet, the Holistic Health Counselor, who helped me years ago with irritable bowel and migraines. I arrived home with the findings of my first trip to Whole Foods. Janet made me an extensive list of thyroid-supportive foods and a couple of supplements that she recommended I start taking. Natural sources of iodine, like sea vegetables, cod, ingredients for Miso soup, grass-fed dairy and meat, and plenty of produce were packed into the fridge. A greens supplement and a kelp supplement went into the cabinet beside the nearly empty container of synthetic daily vitamins I was taking. Janet made sure I was reminded of the importance of organic, non-GMO, and of balancing my plate. She told me to make the meals "an experience" with my one-year-old son and husband, and be sure to share the food with the baby as he was developing his palate.

As I embarked on this journey of getting re-acclimated with food prep and healthier meals, I questioned it. Would it *really* help me? Was the solution to my hypothyroidism this simple? At that time in my life, I was always expecting things to be complicated, which I believe became a self-fulfilling prophecy. I lacked trust, which also meant I lacked hope.

For the first few weeks, I could tell a difference in my energy. My skin and nails looked better, and I felt stronger.

But soon, the little hope I had would wane as I started experiencing irregularity in my period. This energetic "up and down trend" was something that would continue for a while. The ebb and flow of the body rebalancing requires patience, and this was my first rodeo.

I was getting nearly two periods in one month. Instead of going back to the endocrinologist, I decided to do some research and find an option where I felt like I was addressing the root cause instead of just medicating. I came upon a hormone center about thirty minutes from my house. Online, the facility emphasized woman-centered care and discussed "bio-identical" solutions. I got an appointment and was given a saliva test kit and a blood work panel to be completed before the initial appointment.

When we finally met, the practitioner explained to me that I had had near-complete hormone depletion and was entering early menopause. I couldn't believe it. At thirty years old, I was not expecting that, especially after making the changes I had made over the last month or so. In addition to making changes with food, trying out beginner yoga classes, and taking my son for more walks in the stroller, I was reading every book I could get my hands on when it came to thyroid and hormone health.

The practitioner at the hormone center didn't provide what I was expecting. She gave me a bio-identical birth control pill, Armour thyroid, and progesterone cream. This was still a matter of slapping on a band-aid, when I really wanted something more root-cause oriented. Reluctantly, I took the prescriptions and filled them. The temporary good news here is that I entered an upswing as my periods regulated and my energy came back online. I still continued with all the nutritional recommendations from Janet. I was feeling hopeful as I felt a shift in my body, mind, and spirit. And with that, I had a realization about my relationship with God: it had been put on the back burner.

I was asking Him for more at this time, while knowing that I had been doing less on my end. I started reading my Bible again and volunteered to teach Sunday School. I also started engaging in what I call "gratitude walks." I'd take my son, Sully, in the stroller or wagon, and we'd head out on our old country road for some "treasures." He would usually find a rock, feather, leaf, or wildflower to take home with us. I'd be sure to demonstrate to him how we thank God for everything we saw that was good and beautiful. Sully would join in. "Momma, cows! Jesus, thank you!" We were approaching his second birthday, and Sully was continuing to be an early chatterbox. Hearing those sweet words on our walks gave me such great "medicine" on those days.

The more I trained my mind to focus on gratitude and the beauty that was around me at all times, the more I felt the Lord stirring within me. The more I read His words, the more I wanted. It was a craving I hadn't had for a long time. I knew my heart had become hardened by what I had experienced with Sully's traumatic delivery and now experiencing these health challenges. I kept asking God to soften my heart and help me be more open. I wanted to trust Him and hold on to hope.

Lesson #2: Breaking Away from the Pattern of This World and The Deeper Lesson of the Interplay of Food and Spirituality

The early spring of 2015 turned into a hot and humid summer. Just as I thought I was hitting my stride with better eating habits, getting more active, sticking to the Hormone Center's plan, and having the support of a new health coach, Frederick, by my side, my body started to show it wasn't happy again.

Tears of dread and frustration came over me on Father's Day of 2015. I was having a cookout for my family and had started bleeding again. My practitioner at the hormone center had recently changed the dose of progesterone cream, and she also changed my birth control pill. I was certain this was the cause, but I would have to wait until Monday to call. I ended up making an appointment, and when I went in, we discovered that the practitioner had started following the wrong file for me. She had mixed me up with someone else. That's what initiated the change in the pill and cream. I knew at that moment I was done there, and the search would continue. This was a much-needed redirection. I felt God's hand in it. It was from this experience that I learned of the miracle of God's intervention. Instead of disappointment, I felt confident that I was getting closer to finding an answer.

We were camping in early August when I was in the process of weaning from the cream and the pills. Although hopeful, I still struggled with uncertainty. When we were making our three-hour drive home, I went on my phone and started researching "functional medicine" and "holistic nutritionists" in our area. That was when I found the website of the doctor I had been looking for. He is a chiropractic doctor who specializes in holistic clinical nutrition. I read his "pillars of healing," which included nutrition, lifestyle management, and supplementation as parts of the framework. When I entered his office for the first time, there were framed posters on the wall discussing the benefits of various foods, the effects of chronic stress, and notable points on how our food had become so degraded and had much less nutrition due to modern farming practices. My hope soared.

Over the next six months, I would undergo some of the most difficult moments of my journey. I faced some very difficult truths regarding certain relationships, like the one with my mother, the way I managed stress, and, of course, eliminating foods and drinks that showed me how much I was living in my flesh. As I started with the new holistic doctor, I was also receiving guidance and reflection exercises from my health coach, Frederick. He facilitated these discoveries and guided me to take necessary action, and I was searching for Biblical scripture that aligned.

The holistic doctor provided me with an eating plan to reset my gut/gut bacteria, which is a cornerstone in hormonal health. Avoiding wheat, sugar, corn, soy, dairy, caffeine, and alcohol was mandatory for the first three months. It ended up taking me six months to do this elimination diet/detox because I would fall off the wagon and then start over again. Seeing how much of a stronghold these foods and drinks had on me was incredibly eye-opening, and with the help of my health coach, Frederick,

I was able to connect the emotional or energetic depletions to the cravings or desires for certain things.

For example, I wanted coffee because I wasn't getting enough nutrients, hydration, and sleep. The caffeine gave me a false sense of energy; in eastern medicine, they believe that caffeine robs tomorrow's energy for today. It's a vicious cycle that's hard to break. I discovered I wanted sugar when I needed more love and intimacy or when my stress was high, as cortisol (stress hormone) triggers sugar cravings. I craved salt because my minerals were low, which was depleted from pregnancy, and also affected by stress and technology (WiFi, cell phones). I still struggled with wanting to have wine to relax in the evening, when I really needed to be doing a better job managing my stress and taking magnesium, which is a mineral that quells the effects of modern life and helps with sleep.

Having these experiences made me realize how much my spiritual connection to God was influenced by the physical things I was doing. The food, drinks, lifestyle habits, and even products I used in my home were either calcifying and clouding my spiritual connection or strengthening it. That realization became the driving force for staying disciplined and keeping hope that I was on the correct path. Looking back, it was a critical moment in seeing Paul's words from Romans 12 come to life:

> Therefore, I urge you, brothers and sisters, in
> view of God's mercy, to offer your bodies as
> a living sacrifice, holy and pleasing to God—
> this is your true and proper worship. Do not
> conform to the pattern of this world, but be

transformed by the renewing of your mind. Then you will be able to test and approve what God's will is—his good, pleasing and perfect will. (Romans 12:1-2, NIV)

The pattern of this world. The renewing of the mind. I started to see that the food and drinks I became bound to had a pattern or trapping mechanism that did more than irritate my gut or affect my hormones, but also interfered with my connection to God. The physical interference that had been created was feeding spiritual interference. My focus shifted from a concern centered on physical results to protecting my spirit. This was the catalyst for the renewal that was starting in me. That flame grew, and it became easier to resist temptation because I felt the spiritual clarity.

The more aware I became of this, the more disciplined I became in nurturing my body and my family's bodies. The stronger my spiritual connection and discernment became, the more I recognized the sacredness of our physical bodies encasing the Holy Spirit within us. The feedback loop became more apparent as I experienced each new cycle. As Paul says, "Do you not know that your bodies are temples of the Holy Spirit, who is in you, whom you have received from God? You are not your own; you were bought at a price. Therefore, honor God with your bodies" (1 Corinthians 6:19-20, NIV). The changes in food and drink felt like I was peeling or burning away a layer of something that allowed me to not only experience the presence of God on a deeper level but also be more in tune with everyone and everything in my life. It was truly a renewal by fire.

I had a very telling experience of this in the middle of the night during this time. I quickly sat up from my sleep to see a dark, cloaked figure at the foot of our bed. My husband sat up too. No one was speaking, but I had an understanding or a knowing that this was a demonic entity. I understood that I had released it, and that it was leaving in the name of Jesus. When I talked through it with my husband the next day, I told him that it all made sense. Separating from the ultra-processed foods, sugar, chemicals, rancid oils, GMOs, caffeine, and alcohol felt much deeper than just abstaining from food. I had emotional breakdowns, spiritual battles, mental struggles, and after an extended time of being off of it, I did feel a burden leave me.

I believe those battles or struggles with breaking away from what my flesh wanted were a stronger testament to the fact that something nefarious is happening with the production of ultra-processed foods. When you look at the high heat, chemical processes used to create popular packaged foods that people love, these processes kill any energy that's in the food. They create rancid byproducts that produce oxidation in our cells. Couple that with the fact that preservatives and artificial flavorings are added. People are essentially eating empty foods that offer no nutritional value and degrade the building blocks of our bodies. But what about when we eat a fruit or vegetable that's been organically grown? In that case, it's like eating sunshine. The same goes for eating or drinking from animals raised healthfully and provided with all the necessities of a proper environment. There's life and nutrient density in those foods, just as the Lord intended. As much as this is physically healthy for us at a cellular level, it is also spiritually supportive. This is a connection that I would have never made had I not had the health challenges I was experiencing.

The entire process of weaning from unhealthy foods and re-acclimating my system to truly nourishing foods and drinks was like having training wheels on a bike, and then it was time to take them off. I would fall off the bike, and then realize why. Sometimes I'd get going and ride smoothly for a while, only to run into an obstacle or lose my balance again. The more that I made the emotional, mental, and spiritual connections to my lifestyle choices, the more I started to know myself and how to navigate the impulses I would face. This confidence gave me hope for my own health, and it made me realize how this journey I had been on was not in vain. It was the key to rediscovering my relationship with God and with myself. Through that, I realized I wanted to help others "ride their bikes" too.

This is where my health coach, Frederick, encouraged me to get into the same line of work as him. On Christmas Day of 2015, he provided me with a special end-of-year affiliate discount at The Institute for Integrative Nutrition. He told me that with my teaching background and big heart, it made perfect sense to help others achieve the breakthrough I was experiencing for myself. I enrolled and started in January of 2016, which would be one of the most significant years of my life.

Lesson #3: Freedom and Peace: The Gifts of Surrendering

It's not an exaggeration to say that my time at the Institute for Integrative Nutrition (IIN) was life-changing. From the very first lecture by founder Joshua Rosenthal, I was brought to tears. He spoke of concepts like "fitting out" and "dehypnotizing" ourselves from systems or paradigms. Everything we discussed, read, listened to, and applied to our Integrative Nutrition Health Coach training centered upon the fact that we are spiritual beings in a physical world, where many of the systems in place don't foster our spiritual health. That's why so many individuals battle addiction, depression, anxiety, emotional eating, etc. These discussions related to the scripture I had been reading, and I found this to be a stronger confirmation that the answers really were simple. The message was clear. God's intention for our health and well-being is powerful, but it's simple. The complication was the pattern of this world; the systems in play and their focus upon money and power.

As I was in the thick of a refining season in my own faith and spirituality, my husband and I were hoping to grow our family. This was the biggest reason I wanted to reclaim my health, and the more I learned, the more I trusted the Lord. The more I trusted the Lord, the more I allowed myself to feel present in my life and envision our family growing. I also started seeing food as both medicine and art and rediscovered the joy and creativity of it right along with my husband and son. We had planted a garden in May of 2016, and my son loved to pick greens or beets and then see them become part of our meals. We also started juicing and making smoothies.

As I became more obedient to God through my new lifestyle and feeling more present, I felt empowered to take action that showed my true surrender. I began to wean off the thyroid medicine I was still taking. I had been feeling so good that I was almost hyperthyroid, and when I asked the doctor, he said you're on a small dose, so you can try to go without and see what happens. I knew my body was changing for the better, and God gave me the confidence to go for it. After praying and lamenting, it felt right. The next action in letting go was to stop hyperfocusing on my labs.

For almost two years, I was getting constant blood work or doing saliva testing. As I became more confident in my understanding of the body, I also learned that things like lab work are "snapshots" of what's happening inside us. The body is constantly changing, and every process is fluid. People typically see a lab result as concrete or fixed, but in reality, something like thyroid numbers can vary significantly depending on the current phase of a woman's monthly cycle, the level of stress someone is experiencing, and the foods and drinks they consume.

As I started to adopt this mindset shift, I realized I had been stressing myself out about lab results, and it was futile. That was the next step of surrendering. Once again, after prayer and further research, I decided to take a break from the labs. My spirit was at ease, and I felt like a weight had been lifted. The worrying and incessant need to feel in control had been fading, while a newfound peace was filling those spaces. I felt like the Lord was making space for something new.

It was November 2016, and my period was several days late. I had the familiar feeling that I had when I found out I was pregnant with my son. I was more tired than usual and would have bouts of feeling flushed and then a little bit chilled. As the country was awaiting election results that evening, I was getting dinner ready and waiting for that little test stick to give a plus or a minus.

When it was time, I checked and immediately saw the plus sign. I gasped and put my hand to my mouth. I remember just staring at the test stick for a couple of minutes in utter shock and then bursting into tears of joy. I put my hand on my belly and just cried. My husband could hardly believe it when I told him. It was surreal. Throughout the evening, we'd just look at each other and shake our heads with big smiles on our faces. We were like little kids who couldn't sleep on Christmas Eve.

Our daughter Celia will be 9 in July. Since the age of 3, Celia has been telling us she remembers coming to us from heaven. So fittingly, her name means "heavenly" in Latin. What we didn't know was that just a year and a half later, we'd discover we were pregnant again with her sister, Brooke. The fulfillment of our belief, our hope in the Lord, had been delivered.

Conclusion

Recommitting to my faith and relationship with Jesus Christ, going outside the box with natural solutions, and most importantly, surrendering myself fully to God and

His intended path, allowed healing to take place. This was not limited to my own mind, body, and spirit but to my husband and our small son. We were all experiencing this journey together.

It started with recreating my relationship with food and other physical aspects of my lifestyle. Then, choosing gratitude renewed my connection with Jesus. Lastly, I discovered the spiritual and energetic components of health I hadn't known before. I had to address the stifled words and emotions I held onto throughout my life that created a physical buildup; an interruption to my internal flow, which contributed to my body not being able to utilize everything it was given. Frederick, my health coach, allowed me to see this. My trauma, stress, and relationship challenges needed to be addressed just as much as my diet, exercise, personal/home care items, and sleep.

When I decided to let go of trying to control outcomes and just enjoy the process of taking care of myself and my family, I felt a flush of ease take over. The Lord had been inviting me to stop holding on so tightly. Until I was truly obedient to Him, that peace hadn't come. The more I obeyed, the more I would have the words "Trust Me" or "Trust the process" in my mind throughout the weeks of the spring and summer of 2016. And so I did. I kept releasing my worries little by little and just focused on doing the work. The rest was up to Him, and I trusted his provision. I chose to focus on "what *could* happen" instead of "what might *not* happen."

Even though I learned to let go of the possible outcomes of my actions, I worked very hard at the actions themselves in renewing my health. It was a combined effort of taking consistent action and laying my concerns or expectations at the feet of the Lord. Ultimately, I learned to view my life as an offering to God. If I were glorifying Him in everything I was doing, then nothing could technically go wrong. If I didn't get what I wanted out of it, it didn't matter because He was glorified.

I became more present with my family and allowed myself to experience joy and peace instead of dwelling in fear and anxiety. Loosening my grip, allowing myself to feel things completely, and being present were necessary to the physical, mental, and spiritual flow that needs to exist in order to be well. Experiencing the fullness of life required me to set boundaries or even give up certain things that serve as distractions or sources of negativity. Sometimes we have to change careers or relationships, but in those reductions and changes, we create space for what is meant for us.

Only through our Savior and Lord Jesus can we receive the strength and wisdom to do that. God doesn't want us to operate in fear, as he says hundreds of times in the Bible, not to be afraid. Nothing fruitful comes from worry or fear, but everything good comes from gratitude and making space for the peace and possibilities that God desires for us. If someone is walking through their own battle with this, my encouragement would be to make more time to hear God's voice. This world is noisy, and others' opinions or advice are always in our faces because of social media. Seeking quiet time, reading the Bible, or taking prayer walks are great ways to hear God's voice. Changing our focus from what *we want* to being thankful for what *we already have* creates more opportunities for God to bestow joy and peace upon us.

Next Steps

Gratitude is a pillar of health and well-being, supported by research. Expressing our thankfulness is a joyful song to God's ears and is healing for us on every level. When we adopt an attitude of thankfulness in our everyday lives, abundance in the mind, body, and spirit follows. Speaking or writing of our gratitude in prayer is very powerful for us and for our relationship with Jesus.

Daily gratitude journal: List three things you are thankful for each day. This can be done first thing in the morning or at the end of the day.

If you want to include younger children in this, then create a dry-erase gratitude board in a central location or even the children's bedroom. Write down three or more things each day that everyone is thankful for. Watch the gratitude flow and everyone be blessed by it!

Chapter 6

Hope in the Day-in and Day-out: Raising Siblings as Best Friends

By Melanie Wamhoff

"MAY THE GOD OF HOPE FILL YOU WITH ALL JOY AND PEACE IN BELIEVING, SO THAT BY THE POWER OF THE HOLY SPIRIT YOU MAY ABOUND IN HOPE."
—ROMANS 15:13, ESV

I was living in an apartment with five other women. Sounds like a trainwreck, doesn't it? We didn't think so because we had nearly everything in common: we were believers in Christ and physically and emotionally healthy people. Some of us overlapped in our classes, majors, or campus jobs. We were tight. And we had every reason to believe we would remain close because we had lived together for years already without conflict. So, as we began our final year of college together, we looked ahead with great anticipation. We hoped to mimic a family as we gathered for meals, study sessions (well, at least a few!), Bible studies, movie nights, cookie-baking, and spontaneous Pinochle games. We drafted a cleaning schedule for expectation management. Everything seemed perfect for solid, continued friendships under our roof. However, despite our commonalities, history, and plans, divisions formed. Instead of being a unified household, by the year's end, we looked more like hotel guests passing each other in corridors. Graduation Day ended our educational journey and most of our friendships as well.

What went wrong? Upon reflection, now over thirty years later, I see that we lacked intentionality. It didn't occur to us that we needed to keep our eyes on our priorities. While we professed Christ, we were not solidly grounded in Scripture for the foundation of our friendships. We weren't allowing the Word of God to inform our behaviors or thoughts toward one another. When relationships started to unravel, we didn't know to look to other groups of women for counsel or examples. We blindly just lived the way that seemed right at the time. In the end, our situation looked like a worldly one, with self-interests reigning over all else.

Considering these painful losses of roommate friendships from college, I pessimistically wondered, "Is it possible to have unity under one roof? In my future family, could we raise children who are friends, especially girls?"

I recalled a conversation with a college friend, Rachel, who had not been a roommate, someone so sweet, I introduced her to my parents once.

"FOUR SISTERS?" my dad exclaimed. "Wow, you must have fought over the bathroom!"

"Oh, no, we weren't allowed to fight!" Rachel emphatically replied. It was as if my world came to a screeching halt. Her words echoed in my mind: *weren't allowed to fight, weren't allowed to fight ...*

Society speaks of sibling relationships with words of resignation, like "Pretend you like each other" or "they're brothers [or sisters], of course they fight." Sometimes it's "fight it out!" with a faint hint of optimism that one day, kids will figure it out. And from the siblings themselves, "I hate my sister," "my brother is stupid," or, most commonly, "they are annoying."

Rachel's words lingered with me because they were fiercely counter-cultural. And her family lived them out! One day, her sister stopped by her apartment while I was visiting. A quick rap at the door, and Rachel hastily answered. What genuine excitement! Kind words were easily exchanged. Their interaction was natural but intentional, displaying a sweet, enduring friendship. Whenever Rachel spoke of any of her sisters, I fully believed they were the best humans on earth. This was the ideal. How did their parents do this?

Rachel's parents built a firm foundation for their family in Christ. They treasured the Scriptures, talked about them, lived in obedience to them, and centered their lives around them. I could have been completely intimidated by their high bar, but my desire to learn from them trumped the temptation to give up before trying. In John 17:17, Jesus prayed to the Father, "Sanctify them in the truth; your word is truth" (ESV). Sanctification means growing in likeness to Christ. Through the Word of God, they acted like Jesus toward other people. Rachel's family was Christ-like in their love for each other, even in the sibling relationships.

This incredible model fueled my desire to be rooted in Christ and to raise my kids to be close friends, too. It was not at all a reaction to a troubled childhood. I had an idyllic upbringing with both parents and a younger brother. I enjoyed safety, provision, tranquility, health, stability, and solid relationships. I'm very grateful for a beautiful childhood. While my brother and I mostly got along, with three years between us, we had separate interests. We had a spat here and there, but it wasn't awful. Well, except for that one time when we met in the hallway, threw punches, and retreated to our rooms. But, since discussions about Jesus weren't part of the fabric of my childhood home, we didn't have relationships rooted in Christ. There certainly wasn't the vocabulary for it. Maintaining peace was the driving force, not obedience to God.

By God's grace, I had many adult believers in my orbit as a child. I attended a local church's weekly youth club, which included a family-style dinner. Two "table parents" were assigned to a group of kids for the year. I carefully observed my table parents and the rest of the adults of the church, taking mental notes about the Christian lifestyle. Bible study was also part of the weekly meeting. During those lessons, my heart was drawn to Jesus. With an appetite to learn about the Lord and His Word, I became an active member of the Church and continued studying admirable believers. A tremendous gift of mentorship was bestowed upon me in high school, growing my desire for a truly Christian household as I looked toward adulthood.

These wonderful models drove my decision for a Christian college, followed by marriage to a man who treasured Christ.

With faith in Christ and examples always at the forefront of my mind, my husband and I raised our kids with a mindset like Rachel's family's. We *did* wind up with a bunch of girls in our family ... three daughters followed by one son. We are extremely thankful that our four grown children have beautiful friendships with each other, and they always have. Even with ten years between the eldest and the youngest, they have a special bond. We didn't parent perfectly, and our kids certainly had their disagreements. Even though we are all flawed humans, our kids are best friends.

A Reason for Hope: Real Examples Exist

You, too, can hope that your children will be friends because it's a true reality for many families. Since my husband's job moved our family a dozen times as we raised our children, we had the privilege of meeting hundreds of families. In every single new church, we found at least one other family whose parenting served as a great model for us. We observed many relationship-building habits and worked to emulate them.

If you, too, seek families who are raising kids who love each other genuinely, you will find some. Seeing these relationships in action will give you a lot of hope for yourselves.

Here are some common traits of families that were examples to us.

A. Parents anticipate a future friendship with their kids. They don't view their kids as projects or peons. There is no 18-year commitment mindset. Kids are precious family members who will one day be like peers to the parents—dear, life-long friends.

B. Parents prioritize training the hearts of their kids, not just their behaviors. They teach their kids to cherish the gospel, which influences their behavior. If they are being taught to recognize their selfish thoughts and bring them before the Lord who forgives, they cherish grace. And when imperfect people who treasure redemption live together, they are apt to overlook the faults of others. They believe the best about people. And their sibling relationships benefit.

C. Parents don't make comparisons between kids. And they certainly don't pit kids against each other by saying, "Be more like your brother." They don't set them up for competition, either. Hyper-competitive homes may be filled with scholars and athletes, but how are their friendships? Are the siblings all close? Comparisons breed envy. And our society just expects people to be envious. When our middle daughter was getting married six months after her younger sister, we were often asked, "Does it bother your daughter that her younger sister is getting married before her?" It never crossed our minds, and it never crossed hers, either. She was just happy for her sister. Comparing doesn't benefit anyone; God has unique plans for individuals.

D. Parents speak respectfully about their kids and to their kids. This is critical because kids are imitators. When they are with their siblings, they will surely parrot their parents. Therefore, parents who serve as great role models don't mock, slander, or gossip about their kids. This also means they don't complain about their kids. They don't say their child is "in a mood," "driving them crazy," or "a pain in the neck." While it's natural for mothers to seek potty training tips from a more experienced mom, it's for the benefit of learning. Parents ask each other for advice on plenty of things, but I'm not talking about that. It's unhelpful when parents habitually disrespect their children at playdates by whining about their kids' behavior. Mocking kids by mimicking their behavior to make a point or embarrass them is not practiced either.

Parents display respect to their kids with a kind, calm tone of voice. It's the same kindness they extend to friends, coworkers, and strangers. Kids follow the parents' lead in speech and conduct.

A Reason for Hope: Parents Shape Their Kids' Thinking

We can have hope for our children to be friends because we have the privilege and responsibility of shaping their thinking. While each child's unique composition and thoughts are valued and encouraged, God's perfect design demands training by parents. It comes pretty naturally for us to instruct about safety when crossing the road or when nearing a stove. Subtle, societal norms come easily too, like "Wait your turn in line" or "Don't stare at people." Our deeply planted preferences surface for our kids, too, like, "a juicy burger is way better than a dry, overcooked, poor excuse for a piece of beef." But when it comes to the more intricate life lessons, it takes true effort and intentionality to instruct wisely. Proverbs 22:6 says, "Train up a child in the way he should go..." (ESV), so we don't let nature take its course or rely on a child's self-discovery. We have a job to do, especially considering the human heart is deceitful (Jeremiah 17:9). How do we influence the way children think? We talk about the Scriptures "when [we] sit at home and when [we] walk along the road, when [we] lie down and when [we] get up..." (Deuteronomy 6:7, NIV). We instruct our kids in wisdom through conversations as much as possible. How often do we influence their perspectives about their siblings?

Here are some examples of conversations that we had with our kids that shaped their thinking about faith and their relationships:

We started telling our kids that they were going to be best friends the minute they found out a baby was coming. The kids anticipated their "new best friend" with much excitement. The sibling was not going to be a burden who took away their mom's attention; she was going to be a new best friend. We defined the relationships for them.

Every relationship benefits from spiritual growth. When driving home from Bible study, we explained to our kids the Biblical truths we learned that day. Perhaps these conversations were the most beneficial for our kids throughout their whole childhoods. Whatever truth we were excited about, we shared it with them. Because God's Word is living and active, it worked on their little hearts as well as ours.

A subtle way to prioritize sibling relationships came with conversations about sharing. Rather than seeking to keep the peace or to be fair, sharing was the way to exhibit love for each other. We chose those words carefully: "let's let your brother have a turn with the toy now because we love him," instead of "give the toy to your brother because it's his turn."

We help them think about the joy they find in each other. One day, as I was sitting on a bench with one daughter, another was playing nearby on a giant exercise ball. She was bouncing on top of it and having the time of her life. I turned to the one next to me and said, "Don't you love to hear your sister laugh?"

"Yeah, especially because she's so happy," was her reply. My heart swelled. I'm not sure that my young daughter would have realized that she enjoyed her sister's happiness on her own. Our conversation solidified her awareness that she loves seeing her sister happy.

Learning sympathy is critical for close sibling relationships. Observing people around us and discussing situations leads kids to think outside of themselves. It develops their character both outside and inside the home. If we saw a stranger in distress, like an ambulance responding or a woman crying in her car at a stoplight, we talked about it. "What should we do? Let's pray for her." We had conversations like this to teach our kids to have sympathy for other people.

Our care for others did not change with the calendar. Birthday parties were special, and we hosted guests. That did not mean that we loved our guests less on our "special day," turning it into a self-centered spectacle. We talked with our kids about hosting, greeting others at the door, taking their piece of cake after others were served, and honoring the needs of dear friends who had blessed us with their presence. The practice of serving and enjoying others only added to the joy of the special day.

As we drove places, it was time to talk. If we were driving to a youth group, we would ask about who might feel lonely in the group. How could we help include them? If we were invited to a sleepover, we discussed keeping that quiet in case someone else wasn't invited. If others had hard things going on, how could we encourage them? These conversations taught our kids how to think about how their actions impact others. It gave them ideas on how to love well, too, and that translates into sibling relationships. When our son was old enough to attend a youth group, he hitched a ride with his older sister. I missed the time in the car with him until he came home one night and said, "I don't know why, but my sisters like to 'feed me the wisdoms' when they drive me." How grateful I was to hear that his sisters cared about their brother enough to help him grow in understanding, too.

Thinking about siblings in loving ways for all those years translated very easily to someone outside the family. When one of our daughters learned that she was going to have a college roommate from Malaysia, the whole family was excited to welcome her. Since she did not have any friends or family in the United States, our kids jumped at the opportunity to welcome her. She literally became family to us, with her own Christmas stocking, plane ticket for vacation, and regular seat at the dinner table—all the things any family member would have. We don't teach our kids to hold each other in high esteem so that we are insular; rather, we value each other highly because it's God's call for us.

A Reason for Hope: God Calls Us to Obedience

Most importantly, we can have confident hope in raising our kids to be friends because the Scriptures call us to. 1 John 4:20 brings a striking warning: "If anyone says, 'I love God,' and hates his brother, he is a liar; for he who does not love his brother whom he has seen cannot love God whom he has not seen" (ESV).

We can fully rely on the veracity of the Word of God. And what God calls us to do, He also equips us to do. Hebrews 13:20-21 states, "Now may the God of peace ... equip you with everything good that you may do his will, working in us that which is pleasing in his sight, through Jesus Christ" (ESV). It is He who works in us, who gives us all the good things like wisdom, and who enables us to do His will. His grace is sufficient for us to abound in every good work (2 Corinthians 9:8).

When we don't understand God's call to obedience and His power working in us, our relationships won't flourish. Even if we are living under the same roof and having everything in common, solid relationships require more, as my college roommates and I learned. Our cultural norms don't point us in an optimistic direction, either. But there is hope! There are people out there who, by God's grace, are raising kids who are close friends! Find them and follow their example! Watch how they prioritize God's Word and let it inform their relationships. Study how they teach their kids to think wisely. Seek to honor God in obedience and display that for your kids. Intentionally pursue close relationships between your kids for God's glory. And may you, one day, enjoy being best friends with your kids, too.

Next Steps

Journal questions to ponder:

1. Is my home grounded in Christ? Do we allow the Scriptures to inform our relationships?

2. How can I help my children's relationships move forward?

3. Are there parents I would like to learn from as examples in my parenting?

4. What do I think about? How can I retrain my thinking?

5. How do I prioritize obedience to God?

6. How can I shape my kids' thinking?

7. Think about phrases often said in your home. What positive or negative fruits are those phrases bearing?

The Mirror and My Hope

By Anna Gall

If there is a chapter in my life that I could erase, or at least rewrite, it would be this one. But God is all-knowing. He is the Alpha and the Omega, the beginning and the end of my story. That will be the same with your story as well. For me, it turns out to be a major chapter in my story. Many years ago, I found myself in an unsafe situation. I didn't realize it at the time, but I would learn some life lessons along the way and in the years after. I had some emotional and spiritual growing up to do. I had to learn to be people-smart and trust the Holy Spirit to guide me.

I had just started a new job. After about three months of employment, one of the supervisors scheduled a "happy hour" event. It was the day before a holiday weekend. We were all released by midafternoon. I chose to go, knowing the neighborhood establishment was close by, and I wouldn't have too far to go to get home by dinner time. My husband was working late that evening, but the kids would need something for dinner. Besides, I was not planning to stay long. One drink and an appetizer, maybe shoot some pool.

The supervisor ordered drinks and an appetizer platter for everyone. Within a few minutes, I felt woozy from just one drink. Pool shooting was a challenge, and I became a spectacle with my colleagues laughing at me as I stumbled from one side of the pool table to the other. We finished a couple of games, and the same supervisor asked if he could drive me home. I agreed, thinking in my confused mind that this would be best. Turns out this man had more than drinks and pool playing on his mind. I never would have guessed that based on the friendship I thought we had developed.

Memories of the sexual assault were sketchy. I am not a regular drinker, but one alcoholic beverage would not have caused me to pass out. As what appears to be a date-type drug wore off, an overwhelming sense of shame came over me. Following the incident was shock, dissociation, and placating the perpetrator due to fear. In the process of explaining the incident to three people whom I thought I could trust, their insensitivity and curt responses left me with feelings of being victimized again. I talked to these three people within a week following the incident, and each downplayed the assault incident.

I experienced a drastic personality change, and promiscuous behavior was displayed in the few days following the initial assault. I cannot explain this other than I read much later after the fact that these changes can be symptomatic of victims of sexual assault. The choice I made to give in to the abuser during his second approach is where I felt I sinned. My justification was that I was already ashamed, and my husband did not care.

My husband's words after the first incident were, "Do what you have to, so you keep your job. You had better not quit that job!" A threat, not a normal response from a spouse. But then my husband had many of his own issues. The holes in the doors of our house from his fists during fits of unexplainable rage spoke terror. In my mind, all around it was less fearful and painful to give in to this supervisor.

An About Face

Immediately after the second incident, I felt the presence of God Himself. He clearly spoke to me and said, "Listen to me now. There will be consequences for what you have done. Stay away from that man; he is bad company. Stop this behavior. I am with you every step of the way." I simply had a choice to make: continue in this sinful deception or do an about-face, a true repentance.

Once I heard from a sermon that true repentance is like the military command "about face," which is a 180-degree turn from the direction one was headed. I had more fear of being separated from God's love due to sin than the fear of man. I was like the Samaritan woman whom Jesus talked with at the well. He spoke to me with guidance and yet loving acceptance. I did not want to be a disobedient child of God. I could have been the prodigal child, "Father, I have sinned against heaven and in your sight, and am no longer worthy to be called your (daughter)" (Luke 15:21, NKJV). In the ugliness of my sin, I experienced the grace only Jesus provides.

Holy scripture reminds us to confess our sins to one another. After the second incident, and my turning towards our God, I confessed the sin to someone who would help me, not condemn me. I found a professional Christian counselor. Typically, a trusted resource could be a friend, family member, pastor, and/or faith-based counselor who will keep confidence, give guidance, and pray with you towards healing. The counselor I chose allowed me to talk, and she listened to me. My professional helped me build self-confidence and trust my own instincts. "You are going to learn how to take care of you," she said at our first session. Some people may fail to understand your confession and will condemn you instead. It would be a while before I spoke to a pastor, and he extended grace and forgiveness to me after listening to my story. I felt this pastor represented the heart of God the Father and Jesus. "But where sin abounded, grace abounded much more" (Romans 5:20b, NKJV).

In the weeks ahead, I made it clear to this harassing supervisor to stay away from me. I became a nervous wreck, not knowing how he would behave and what the work environment would hold each day. This man would harass and ridicule me in front of my co-workers. Quickly, I lost thirty pounds in a matter of a few weeks. I had a few extra pounds on me to start with, so I did not appear to have an eating disorder to the outside world. My counselor didn't think I would make it through a trial if I chose to prosecute. The counselor recommended a psychiatrist who ordered antidepressants. Not receiving encouragement to deal with the assault face-to-face at this time, I stuffed the details of those memories into the dark recesses of my mind. Those details were sealed for over twenty years.

The talk therapy sessions at that time were about my childhood, marriage, relationships, and taking care of myself. I learned to listen to my own instinct. I left the hostile work environment for better employment despite my husband's threats. My own well-being became the priority. To my husband, children, and parents, I may have appeared very self-centered and self-absorbed at times. My priorities now included myself, not just them. I was finally taking care of myself, getting stronger on the inside each day. The prescribed antidepressants delay what eventually is opened and exposed, the sexual assault and my sin.

Trust In God First

My personal relationship with God is my foundation. Trust in Him first, then the God-given skills of counselors and helpers along the way. Watch for helpers along your journey that minister to the whole person—spiritual, physical, mental, emotional, and vocational. For me, practical steps such as obtaining my bachelor's degree gave me confidence in other important decisions for my life. Making time to improve vocational skills, obtaining certificates or advanced education, and joining a bible study were healthy choices. At times, these steps to personal growth and improvement seem tedious. "First steps always seem like not enough, but they are the bravest, and they start the journey to where you're meant to go. It takes great trust to believe in the smallest of beginnings,"[5] author Ann Voskamp encourages in her writings.

There were consequences from what happened so many years ago and dealing with the assault memories along my journey to healing. Humility was my reminder that I am from dust and will leave earth that way. But by Jesus' blood, the love and grace of God win over death. Facing those once-covered memories head-on is part of the healing journey. "You can't appreciate how far you have come … unless you know where you have begun."[6] Overcoming fear is an ongoing, everyday battle.

My True Identity

I am freed by recognizing the truth of God's Word, the true mirror. Promises in God's Word keep me grounded. I read God's Word and meditate on His Word. I leave notes of affirmations in my purse, on the bathroom mirror, in my vehicle's dashboard, and on my work computer. I focus on that true mirror and my hope in Jesus. This is my true identity.

For those who endure trauma, reality can come in glimpses or full screen. It is by God's grace and how much one person can bear at any given moment. Some deal with trauma like a stage play, one scene, and one act at a time.

---

5   Voskamp, Ann. *The Broken Way: A Daring Path to the Abundant Life.* Grand Rapids, Michigan, Zondervan, 2016, 75.

6   Laura Ingalls Wilder, and Stephen W Hines. *Words from a Fearless Heart : A Collection of Wit, Wisdom, and Whimsy.* Nashville, T. Nelson Publishers, 1995, v-vi.

This would be how my memories and life unfolded. The trauma I experienced cannot be viewed all at once. Reading God's Word and inspirational books, journaling, writing, gardening, the creative and culinary arts, and faith-based therapy have become my sanity and path to wholeness.

Last year, while visiting the Pompeii display at a local museum, I read an ancient scholar's description of the town of Pompeii being covered completely with volcanic flames and ashes. It was not discovered for over 1600 years. "Not the darkness of a cloudy night or a night where there is no moon, but darkness as if the light had gone out in a room that is locked and sealed,"[7] This describes the kind of darkness that my sexual assault memories went into. My life was once covered in layered walls of dirt and soot. For my stronger self, the memories of the assault would leak out through a pinhole one at a time. It would be years before my understanding of what sexual trauma syndrome, post-traumatic stress disorder, and chronic stress syndrome developed.

My career development requires reading books on business and personal improvement. I learned that in Japan, there is a change process called kaizen, which means to place one foot in front of the other. This concept, when applied, works wonderfully for business, relationships, and health practices. My healing came one step after another. For a year, a physical separation from my husband came before the inevitable divorce. In my heart, the lack of protection and covering from my spouse severed the trust needed for our marriage to survive. My

---

7   Pliny the Younger. "Pompeii: The Exhibit," St. Louis Science Center. 2025.

husband did not want to seek counsel for our marriage's survival. The divorce was uncontested.

With divorce, at some point forgiveness is required for a person to move on and heal. "... if anyone has a complaint against another; even as Christ forgave you, so you also must do" (Colossians 3:13, NKJV). I learned to give that gift of forgiveness to my ex-husband. But also, for myself, I gave that forgiveness to the sexual assault perpetrator and the persons who failed me when I was most vulnerable. I had to be patient in my relationships as well as with myself. The words, "I forgive you," may come before the emotions do. Forgiveness is a choice and a process. For you, this process may be different from mine. But essentially, forgiveness frees your mind and heart from making a person indebted to you. You are free to be completely who God wants you to be. Jesus provides that ultimate example of forgiveness.

My true identity is found in Jesus. I recall again and again who I am in Jesus, not what others say. His Word is my mirror. We all know how people talk, and rumors run rampant. I did and still overcome guilt by the blood of Jesus. He has removed my sins from me "as far as the east is from the west" (Psalm 103:12, NIV). Joy returns to me, seen in my healthier relationships and wholesome activities. After my divorce, I kept studying God's word, joined a Christian singles' group, and volunteered at church and community events.

My daily walk is with that kind of hope I have in Jesus. He warms my heart and gives me a new life. Keeping up with my family, a tight budget, and multiple jobs is challenging. Resilience is a by-product of the hope I have in Jesus. God is faithful to meet me where I am, even without a husband after twenty-six years of a failed marriage. The Holy Spirit is my calming presence. My physical health improved as I was taking better care of myself. Eventually, I received a job promotion with my primary place of employment, which allowed me to work just one job.

Some matchmaking by a friend was going on unbeknownst to me. I was introduced to a good Christian man about three years after the divorce from my first husband. This wonderful man, my soulmate, has a similar background to mine. We married one year after our courtship. Not a perfect relationship, but we love each other, work on the relationship together, and protect one another. Our marriage is not without the challenges of our previously troubled past and the balance of our blended family of six adult children and ten grandchildren. Our home has fostered displaced pets from time to time. Shared interests in history, antiques, plants, birds, music, serving, and fundraising for the less fortunate keep us busy between visits with family.

Due to my previous experiences, trust in my relationships is an area of continual growth. My comfort zone is narrow. I must call on the Holy Spirit for discernment and take one step at a time. People will fail because no one is perfect. Others fail and do not care who they hurt along the way. The careless, heartless, and malicious individuals are those whom I especially pray for, for their spiritual salvation first and foremost. It is that hope in Jesus that I cling to for my safety, my health, my marriage, my other relationships, and what endeavors God has called me to.

Without a doubt, I know nothing will separate me from the love of God. If God can love me at my worst, He can and will love anyone and everyone. I can rejoice and give God thanks for His faithfulness to me, like the Samaritan woman for a brief period so many years ago. He meets me where I am. He shows me His heart. By His grace, I trust Him to hold me and then guide me as I walk this life. Anyone living in sin can do an about-face towards God, accept His forgiveness, and forgive oneself because of Jesus' example, the ultimate gift of hope.

Next Steps

I pray you, "Make that a 180-degree turn from the sin that you are entangled in. Walk into the arms of Jesus, who forgives you. Forgive yourself as God guides you, and you will walk into new life with our Savior, Jesus Christ. Amen."

Chapter 8

A Hope Story Brought Out of Darkness

By Elisa Rendon

My story is a story of redemption and dependence on the mercy of God. I knew the Lord at 15 years of age. I was in an evangelical church until I was 22 years old, when I left because of conflicts that arose, which sorely disappointed and hurt me. Being so young, I lacked the sense to navigate those troubled waters with Jesus.

Fast forward a few years, and I was sitting in a psychiatrist's office getting diagnosed with a mental disorder. It was the beginning of a long journey that would take me into my forties before I returned to Jesus, having gained the understanding that my life without Him was a voiceless struggle.

I survived taking many overdoses, although the first one left me reeling with distress and cognitive impairment. Before that, I had worked as an Interpreter. Now I could not balance a checkbook or do a simple sum. My doctor did all the paperwork, and six months later, I began receiving disability payments. The answer to the paperwork came much sooner. Six weeks after they were submitted, I was declared to be disabled.

Being declared to be disabled was blunt and shocking. I had always worked. I felt terribly alone in this new reality. My marriage was on the rocks, and my husband resented my disability and that I would no longer work for a good salary. Also, I had a young child whom I loved very much. The one smart thing I was capable of thinking was telling him that if mommy was crying or screaming, it wasn't his fault. It was because mommy had an illness. My son was to see me through withdrawal of medications, and because of that, I knew he would not succumb to taking drugs because he knew firsthand the incredible anguish withdrawal brought.

At that time, at 40 years of age, I found out I was expecting again. I was terrified. When my son was conceived, a charismatic Catholic priest had prayed for me and over my unborn child. At this time, when I was expecting again, I was taking medicines that were very strong. The obstetrician had me speak to a genetic counselor at the hospital where the baby would be born. Her words ran loud and clear. I could not function without the medicines, and in order to care for my baby, I needed to function. Therefore, the medicines were necessary. Thankfully, they did not pass through the placenta, so my baby was sheltered from them.

My daughter was a blessing from God. Since I was home, I had the time with her that I'd not had with my baby boy. Her joy was infectious. When she was a little over a year and a half old, I bought watercolor paints, crayons, and poster boards. She and I splattered paint all over them. At the time, there were these videos that were called Baby Einstein, and I watched them with her. They were beautiful, with startlingly lovely images and music. They were made with the thought of stimulating a child's perceptions and imagination. To me, they also spoke of great beauty.

My son loved his baby sister passionately. He went to school each day and told the class about all that was happening at home. Even my husband was enchanted with her, and that made my life easier, as he was less likely to lash out at me in anger. I felt very lonely without female friends. All the friends I'd had at work disappeared. My husband would not allow me to go to an evangelical church because he was brought up Catholic and believed evangelicals were heretical. My one recourse was YouTube and the songs of Christian artists.

On my way to my mother's house, I would play the cassettes of Christian artists, and my daughter grew accustomed to the songs of praise. Her loving kindness was a gift from God. She was a sweet-hearted child, and she loved me very much. I, in turn, poured all the love of my hungry heart over her and my son, and these children were a lifeline. I learned about the mercy of God from experiencing their constant love. I realized that in spite of my illness, God had given me these children so I could feel his love through them. Caring for them helped me get through each day of living with my husband and suffering through his criticism and veiled violence.

Indeed, God was a merciful God. Although there were other overdoses, brought about by the depression and paranoia, He never left me. He continued to pour His words into my heart. My bruised soul experienced forgiveness and mercy. I learned to look for Him more and more in Scripture and learned that Jesus would carry my burdens (Matthew 11:28-30). Learning that Jesus would always be there for me was a soothing balm to my aching heart.

Although I had attempted suicide multiple times, I never experienced rejection from Jesus. He made sure I understood that Christians were not perfect; they were redeemed. My search through the Scriptures led me to see a God that was a consuming fire, but He was also long in mercy (Psalm 103:8). It was his mercy that soothed me, and although I took many medications for depression, anxiety, and paranoia, I understood He did not blame me for those things I did out of sheer desperation.

Instead, he led me, as Psalm 23 says, by the still waters. I felt Jesus' acceptance and mercy pour into my soul. I learned that Jesus had loved me since He was on the cross and had shed His precious blood to ransom me from my sins. As years passed, I became more dependent on Jesus for everyday living. Although I still could not go to an evangelical church, He gave me the solace of songs of praise. I was His child, despite my multiple flaws and mistakes. In the midst of my pain, I sought solace from other men, always feeling the need from my childhood of being accepted and loved by a man. My father had divorced my mother before I was a year old, and I grew up feeling unloved by men, deserted by the one man who should have stood in place so I could learn fatherly love.

Looking for love in men's faces was an exercise in futility. Not one of those men loved me back or cared for me as a person. I was like a girl in a song I'd heard, looking for love in too many faces and places. Jesus, nonetheless, didn't quit loving me. He waited until I was able to understand that His love for me was eternal and that I didn't have to do anything to earn it. I feel that this is something that He wants each Christian to know. However wrong our actions may be, if we repent and ask for forgiveness, He will forgive us. His love passes all understanding.

His love was freely given. It had always been there. Understanding this truth finally set me free. I no longer felt I needed to earn love. His love was given without conditions, letting me be a new person in Him. This realization, when it finally took place, freed me from the lonely heart looking for acceptance because it felt it had been abandoned. Indeed, realizing that Jesus accepted me as I was and would always be by my side, regardless of the mistakes I made, led me to understand redemption. Our asking for forgiveness always brings it about. He sees into our hearts and knows that we are sincere.

I found out He would never leave me or forsake me as He said to Joshua (Deuteronomy 31:6). He delighted in loving me, and I, in turn, began to find delight in seeking His presence, learning joyfully that I was never to fear being abandoned again. It was the greatest story of hope I had ever encountered, certainly one I had ever lived. Jesus was my Savior and the lover of my soul. He accepted me unconditionally. I had never been accepted unconditionally. Understanding that His love was unconditional freed me from the burden of guilt and self-accusation.

I had learned one important truth, one that would never fail. I was redeemed, ransomed from my sins. I was loved without fail. Nothing or no one could ever separate me from the love of Jesus. For the lonely little girl I had carried inside me, this was total and complete joyfulness. Little by little, I learned the "unforced rhythms" of His companionship (Matthew 11:28-30, NJKV). I began hungrily devouring Scripture, Christian books, and devotionals. Everything that taught me about Him was a newfound treasure.

Praying for other people to have the same experience became a ministry He gave me. I wanted other people to know Him as I did. When my daughter was old enough to understand, I taught her how to pray. My own prayer for both my children was for them both to be Christians and not to have paranoia. The Lord, in His mercy, answered both prayers. My son left for the Army at 18 and came back a Christian, having found Jesus in a Christian church. My daughter, as well, prayed and followed the Lord, believing in Him with a full heart. In answer to my prayer, neither of my children is paranoid. Such mercy had the Lord shown me that I would have never expected.

Both my prayers were answered. I had joy in seeing my children embrace the love of Jesus. I had joy seeing in them no trace of paranoia. I felt so blessed and aware of how things were happening through no deed of my own but through the love and mercy of Jesus. That's a truth that is without fail. Nothing I could have said or done would have brought about these blessed happenings. I trusted God, in all truth, but of myself I had no power to bring about the miracle of His love poured into my children's lives, nor spare them from a terrible illness.

I have come to a place where my hair is white, my eyes don't have the same vibrancy as before, and there's arthritis in my knees. As Abraham and Sara, who had to wait until old age before they could have Isaac, I went through a whole lifetime and many ups and downs, in order to come to this place where I find myself (Genesis 21:1-5). I have joy. Joy despite my illnesses. Joy despite disappointments, mishaps, mistakes. Jesus does not look at them. He redeemed me through shedding His blood on a cross. He gave His life so I could be ransomed from my sins.

People ask, "How do you know Jesus is real?" My answer is: because I walk next to Him every day of my life. Because I have seen countless times where He has brought me forward through tumultuous waters. People ask, "Is this not in your mind, as opposed to being a truth?" No. I could not possibly have brought about such faithfulness. My eyes have seen the glory of the Lord, as an old hymn says.

I could have died in one of multiple overdoses. I could have lost the love of my children had they held contempt for me because of those overdoses. I could have seen them disbelieve that there is a true Jesus, after seeing their mother go through withdrawal and suicide attempts.

None of that has happened. They both understand, and they both believe in the unfailing love of Jesus. Even after my husband and I got divorced, they have not stopped loving their parents. They both understand that together we could not make life work for each other because there were many conflicts brought about by our personalities, by misunderstandings.

I questioned after each suicide attempt why I had been left alive. I finally came to understand that God had work left for me to do. This work is understanding that these truths I have learned need to be passed on to other people, be held in my heart and soul, so I can bring about compassion to other people, who may have gone or will go through similar circumstances. There is nothing wasted in the Lord's kingdom. No lesson that is left to waste, no page that is left unturned. The resilience that I have gained in my life through all of my circumstances has helped me to become more understanding, helpful, and compassionate toward those who are in a difficult, stark place.

Moreover, I have become a faithful witness. I have encountered grace, and it is my task to tell other people that God gives them grace and that they must give grace to themselves. I could not have known this unless suffering had polished me like a rock beaten by the waves, brought to be a smooth, rounded surface that avid collectors look after. I would never have fully understood the tears of another if I had shed no tears of my own. And, even though people tell me that this is a lesson, or many lessons, that I could have learned by myself, I know that this is not true.

I would have never succeeded in transforming paranoia into a merciful tool of grace. I would not have been able to help someone love life again after being broken in pieces. These are truths that come to the heart only by the grace of God. They cannot be learned by the exercise of the intellect. They cannot be felt by willing compassion out of a heart and soul that did not have the loving heart of Jesus. How do I know that? Because for years I wandered about without Him in my life. Believing that my intellect and experience could fashion me into an able helper. But nobody can give what they don't have, and I may have had compassion but not the grace of God.

My purpose in writing these words is to make other people understand that nothing, nothing in all creation, can separate us from the love of God (Romans 8:38-39). I want others to know the same love and unconditional acceptance that I received from Jesus. I want them to understand that, however broken, dirty, disgraceful their lives may be, Jesus loves them. He shed precious blood to ransom all of humanity from its sin. And even if we still make mistakes after receiving Him into our lives, if we repent and confess, He forgives us.

If you are reading these words and wondering how it can happen to you in the midst of your own troubles and despair, those which you carry but carefully hide from others, I can only tell you to call upon the name of Jesus and receive His gift of salvation. Be cleansed by that precious love that was shed on a cross. Be blessed by that mercy that knows no limits, that love that is infinite, that grace that is priceless. Call upon the name of Jesus and receive His gift of salvation. Trust that He, having suffered terrible torment and death for us to be ransomed, can come into your heart and soul and transform you into someone new.

Next Steps

Once you receive Jesus into your life, you become a new creation in Him. Seek His presence through reading Scriptures, listening to worship songs, and making prayer an indivisible part of your life. Looking for a church where you can worship with other Christians is important for your growth, spiritually and in knowledge. Sharing with others the words of Scripture will allow you to understand the purpose of Jesus in your life. You will also become part of a community of believers who are not perfect but are redeemed. This will help you to carry out the work Jesus has for you in your life with Him.

Chapter 9

Hope Beyond Loss:
A Journey of Grieving

By Noemi Rivas

I was definitely the "sensitive kid" in my family. If I fell or got hurt, the shock and the memory of it would stay with me for days—I'd basically grieve the accident. My siblings, there were 14 of us, thought I was weird; they had witnessed me fall and get head injuries or get skin burns from an unattended clothing iron. But I think I was just hyper-aware. Even now, I can walk into a room and immediately 'read' the atmosphere of the space before anyone says a word: "... Your rod and your staff protect and comfort me" (Psalm 23:4, NLT).

Do you remember how you responded to pain as a child? Maybe a scraped knee, a harsh word, or the feeling of being left out would linger with you longer than others noticed. Perhaps a small comfort, a gentle hug, or a caring word from someone close would help to bring you back?

Well, for me, as I grew older, life began to hit me from all angles with full force. On one of many occasions, I had a softball accident as a young girl. I began using laughter as a defensive mechanism, having survived so many traumatic events in the past. I went from crying through the pain all the time to laughing off the pain. By the time I was in high school, I had become an expert at laughing off any pain. One day, I was at a JV softball practice doing in-field warmups. The day was quite exciting for me; I'd never played this position before, and I was very nervous. I was trying out for first base for the first time. The sun was warm that day, and the wind was springy. Then everything slowed down, and I could hear my heartbeat in my ears. Suddenly, out of nowhere, *bam*—the ball hits me straight into my left eye. Okay ... Okay, I wasn't paying attention, but honestly, it felt like I was playing with pros!

You know how in those old cartoons, when a character gets hit, all they see are stars? Well, that actually happened to me. I got hit right in the eyeball. As I covered it up, I felt a sting, and it began to swell and turn pitch black, but then I saw little bright shooting stars in my injured eye. In this incident, all I could think of was this Looney Tunes cartoon, and I started laughing. I laughed so hard the girls on my team thought I was crazy. What they didn't know was that I could see stars through my injured eye.

I realized then that the pain became almost non-existent. At least, for part of the day. It wasn't until that evening, after a visit to the ER, that the pain would arrive. But, in that moment, the laughter became my coping mechanism. It became my go-to for any type of pain. I don't know why the Lord gave me this ability, but I imagine it was to prepare me for the difficult moments to come in my life. "... Your rod and your staff protect and comfort me" (Psalm 23:4, NLT).

But I wasn't prepared for what this looked like as an adult. Laughing stopped working for me. How can you laugh sadness away, heartache away, or loneliness away? These were all coming at me at full speed, the way that softball did that time at practice. And now I'm no longer a teenager. I'm a daughter, a new bride ... and soon-to-be a mom? "Even when I walk through the darkest valley..." (Psalm 23:4, NLT).

When laughter was no longer enough, leaning into prayer became essential, and I found comfort in talking honestly with God about my pain. Journaling my thoughts and feelings helped me process what I was going through. I started opening up to close friends, letting them see when I was struggling. Sometimes, simply taking a quiet walk or listening to worship music gave me space to breathe and reset. These new coping strategies made the pain bearable, and they helped anchor me when the waves of sadness came.

It was during this time that Jeremiah 29:11 became my anchor, my life verse. "'For I know the plans I have for you,' says the Lord. 'They are plans for good and not for disaster, to give you a future and a hope'" (NLT). It's funny how this is still relevant: God alone knows His plans for us. The next two verses read, "In those days when you pray, I will listen.

If you look for me wholeheartedly, you will find me. I will be found by you ..." And indeed I needed to look for Him wholeheartedly, not pretending that everything was okay, on the outside, when I was falling apart on the inside.

Our First Anniversary

We were about to celebrate our first anniversary. We were still living like newlyweds, looking forward to being married, enjoying our new married life with all the nuances of married life, of getting used to our likes and dislikes, of getting to know each other's space, and making sure we told each other 'I Love You' as if it was our last time. Everything was beautiful and sunny, and flowers smelled wonderful like a new spring, and birds were singing their song, and the color of the sky seemed more beautiful than ever.

And then we received a call. My sister was on the line, her voice trembling, "Dad's not doing well. We had to admit him to a convalescent home because he'd passed out on the bathroom floor."

Suddenly, my heart slowed down, and I had this pit in my stomach. I found out that he'd passed out because he was dehydrated, and they had to rush him to the hospital. But because of his condition and lack of insurance, they couldn't keep him in the ER, so he was admitted temporarily into a convalescent home, where we later found out my dad had less than two months to live.

This amazing year, in which my husband and I were beginning our new life together. Still remembering the year before, how my daddy walked me down the aisle. *He can't be sick. He was doing so well* ... And now we're just finding out that my dad had been diagnosed with cirrhosis of the liver due to his diabetes. This strong man I grew up admiring, thanking God for his wisdom and for living a surrendered life for the Kingdom of God. He had led many people to the Lord. He was a pastor who loved helping people. He shepherded many people to the cross of Jesus, and he lived out "the Good Samaritan story" before our eyes.

So when the doctor told us, "I only give your father 45 days to live at most, more like a month ...," my heart sank, and I began spending evenings with him after work. During this time, we had been making plans to celebrate our first anniversary. But wait ... "What do you mean, my dad is going to leave us?" All of this was a lot to take in. At first I was afraid, then a little upset, and yeah, I was sad. I was sad that he was leaving us because there was so much I still wanted to say to him. But I knew that I needed to do everything I could for him over the next 45 days. "Even when I walk through the darkest valley, I will not be afraid, for you are close beside me" (Psalm 23:4, NLT).

I knew that I needed to be there for him the way he was there for us. I canceled any plans for our anniversary celebration. And so from there I went into what I'm calling "crazy daughter" mode. Because I needed to take him out of this convalescent home, I needed to get him out of this place. I'd heard in these places you smell death going in and coming out. And although he'd been there a few days, this place seemed to be making him even sadder. What I didn't understand was how bad his condition was. So I tried to get him out by starting to look for a place near my house. There was a senior living home that we were looking at, but it was too expensive for us.

We couldn't afford it, and, of course, he didn't have any more of his retirement pension, having retired at 55. He was born on February 10, 1928, so he was 78 years old when he was diagnosed. We thought for sure he would make it to his 80th birthday, and now he had barely reached 79.

I was just so overwhelmed because he had left behind quite a legacy. I got ahead of this and began calling everybody to visit him, since he didn't have long. He had his ministry in Ensenada, Baja California, Mexico. This town would be the place we were going to take his body for a final burial; it was his final wish to be buried there. He loved this town, the culture, and the community. He loved the people there and the weather. So for his final wish, we were going to honor him.

But before we got to our final goodbye, my husband decided we needed this trip up north for our first anniversary, which happened to be close to the 30-day mark the doctor had mentioned. And because my dad seemed to be doing well, we left my sisters and brother in charge of his care at the convalescent home, and they would let us know if anything happened, we'd turn right back.

Even with all of this, my husband and I had been trying to get pregnant. We had been trying for more than a few months, but because of my dad's health, we just stopped trying for a bit. We ended up deciding, well, actually my husband decided that we were going to take our first anniversary trip after all, all the way up to Monterey, California. My husband had planned it to the T. But my heart and my spirit were not well. Usually, I'm the planner. We're both golfers, and we wanted to see Pebble Beach, even if only from afar because of the price. Despite that, I'm glad we went. I'm glad we visited.

So, we traveled Highway One; for those of you who are not in California and don't know what that looks like, it's a very curvy road along the coast, but it's a beautiful drive up there. The day was sunny and breezy at the same time; you could smell the sea air while the sun was hitting your face. Suddenly, on one of those turns, I felt very nauseous, and I was like, well, I'm driving, so I guess it can't be the road that's making me nauseous. We weren't driving too fast. It was actually impossible. The highway is pretty curvy, so I knew it wasn't my driving. All of a sudden, I told my husband, "I'm going to pull over so you can take over." And he's like, "Oh, okay, are you okay?" and I said, "Yeah, I'm just feeling a little weird, a little dizzy," more than usual, but this was not unusual for me. As a kid, I'd get car sick all the time. But, somehow, I needed to get out of the car because it was getting worse.

I kept thinking this was just weird. Everything was spinning all of a sudden for no reason, or so I thought. I didn't know what it was, and so I composed myself and pulled over. My husband took over the wheel, and we continued, ending up at a place called Big Sur restaurant right off the highway, before continuing to Monterey that night.

So my dizzy spells subsided. The next morning, we ate breakfast, planned our day locally, and went to the aquarium. But right around dinner time, I felt like I needed to go to the pharmacy. We bought a pregnancy test, but it was confusing. It had plus and minus and too many instructions. We didn't get anything from it but an unknown result. So we continued with our evening. The next morning, on our way back from breakfast, it felt like we needed to do another test. I had seen a commercial on a test that just showed the words "pregnant" or "not pregnant." Simple enough. There we were, completely nervous and excited and worried all at once. Then the timer went off. The words kept blinking, saying "not pregnant," then it stopped and said, "Pregnant." And we looked at each other, realizing, we're having a baby!! Oh wow, just saying those words freaked me out. Because reality hit, and my dad was still leaving us soon.

After We Arrived Back Home

I got into my office to start my day after a beautiful 4-day break, while my sisters took care of him for a few days. I had already planned to come and visit my dad that Monday evening. To be by his bedside, I was planning on reading another one of his favorite Psalms. So I was excited this time, felt refreshed, joyful, and rested. On June 11, 2007, I received a phone call from the convalescent home that morning. It was the morning nurse, "Ahh, hi, this is nurse ...Your dad isn't responding; you need to come as soon as you can." I replied, "Are you sure? My sisters said they had come by to see him on the weekend, and he was fine, and he was very chatty." She says, "No, you don't understand. He's not responding to anyone." I hadn't even started my workday. I ran to my boss's office and told her that I had to leave, that my dad wasn't responding. She said, "Go."

And I was still thinking maybe he wasn't feeling well or wasn't having a good day; I'm sure he just needed us to be there by his side. Then I quickly called my sister-in-law, who was a nurse. And I asked her what it means when they say, "He's not responding?" and she said, "Oh, Mimi, this means his breathing is very shallow, and he's about to die." She said, "This happened to my mom." Her mom had passed away from uterine cancer a few years ago, so she was familiar with this phrase.

I immediately went into work mode, called my brother, my sisters, and my husband. I called everyone I could think of, "My dad's not responding, come say goodbye, he's leaving us today." My voice was shaking, and I was trying to find a way to laugh the pain away, but I couldn't! And all the while I was holding my belly because I didn't want any of my pain to reach my womb. I felt that I needed to protect my baby from all of this.

I had read that the first trimester of any pregnancy is the most vulnerable for the mom and the baby. By now, I had seen the doctor, and they had done the sonogram. I found out, yes, I was ten weeks along in my pregnancy. So I was being very careful with what I was eating, drinking, and listening to.

Then I remembered my mom. I tried reaching her, but nobody answered, and I kept calling … no answer. It wasn't like her, she'd always answered. By now, you should know that my dad came to us for help because my mom was caring for her mom. My grandma had gotten a weird diagnosis of a spinal condition that bends it forward. My grandma needed 24 hour care. And my mom was the only one there to care for her. My dad asked her to place him on a bus back to my sister's to care for him so that she could focus on her mother's care. Even then, he wasn't thinking about himself.

Saying Goodbye to My Daddy

It was the hardest and yet the most peaceful goodbye. I made my way into my dad's room. And the next thing I realized was the nurses coming into his room around me. I'd been with my dad plenty of times as a child when he did ministry, and I'd join him to visit the sick or pray for them as they were leaving the earth. I realized that when all the nurses start to surround you, it's because they are waiting for you to fall apart; they want to be there with you, for you. The part that I wasn't expecting was my own reaction to what I encountered in the room.

I had imagined my dad still breathing shallow breaths, lying peacefully; this image gave me peace. But, instead, I found his body in a catatonic state, his body slightly raised and his mouth wide open. But yes, he was still breathing shallow breaths. My heart broke at this moment because it looked like he was suffering. I remember asking the nurse if this was normal, and she said, "Yes ... you can talk to him."

I didn't know what to say. I wasn't ready to say goodbye to him, and then I asked the nurse, "How long could he stay this way?"

She responded, "We don't know, it can be a day or a whole week. It's when he's ready to leave." And, I knew that to die is to be present with the Lord. But when she said this, it made me ask: was he waiting for us to say goodbye? And so, as my family began to arrive to say goodbye. I felt peace in the room and a beautiful warmth. His bed was next to a sliding door, and the sun made its way in like I'd never experienced. I had no fear, no understanding of what was happening. I wanted so badly to cry, but I couldn't. No tears came out. I didn't understand it. So, I comforted other family members, processing that my daddy was still with us. And so we waited.

This moment reminded me of the mournful examples of women in the Bible; this must be what it looked like for them. This went on for a few hours. We arrived at 9 a.m. that morning, and everyone was coming, but my oldest brother and his family were stuck in traffic. It felt like my dad was waiting for him to arrive.

A few minutes later, the nurse checked his vitals and noted that his oxygen levels were dropping slowly. She assured me it would be any minute. My oldest sister was an addict at the time, and she took this very hard. She'd walked away from the Lord years before this. As she sat by his bedside, she asked if they could give him a blanket because he was cold. The nurse insisted he wasn't in any pain or discomfort, but she honored her request and brought a blanket, which she covered him with. The machine kept beeping. The nurse came in to listen to his heart one last time. She said it's slowing down. My brother was still not here. But just watching him in this state was terrible for us. And I kept seeing my sister weep.

You see, my dad, when I was 9 yrs old, he sat with me at a funeral that he ministered in. And we saw how family members would make a spectacle in their grieving by throwing themselves on the casket and screaming. This particular funeral was for a friend of his; she and her husband both loved the Lord. But her family refused to follow Jesus. And we were all just sitting in this chaotic moment. And my dad looked at me and said, "Promise me you won't do this when I die." and I said, "Okay, Daddy, I promise." But I quietly asked, "But can I at least cry?" And then he said, "You can always cry, but don't cause a scene… These women were screaming and throwing themselves on their mom's casket, and they were upsetting the room. They were riddled with guilt and had no convictions of where she was now; she was with her Heavenly Father," he said.

Somehow, this moment with my own sister reminded me of that funeral. I still couldn't understand why no tears came from me. It was almost 2 p.m., and there was no sign of my brother. My dad's oxygen level was getting lower. My sister was still crying. It became the chaotic scene my dad did not want. So … I got up and came next to his ear, and I whispered (in Spanish), "Daddy, it's okay for you to go home now. Go be with Jesus, we will see you soon."

I stepped back. Fifteen seconds later, I saw his face turn from fear to a peaceful grin, and then he took his last breath. Then … he was gone. My sister was louder. Everyone tried to surround her and just let her cry. I walked out of the room onto the patio of his room, and I felt like I couldn't breathe. I just realized he heard my voice and left us. But no tears. Instead I experienced this peace that He was no longer suffering and was in the presence of Papa.

My brother eventually arrived at the news that my dad was gone. He was the son who helped raise our family at one point, a story for another time, but he was always very quiet. My heart broke for him as well, but no tears.

I quickly tried calling my mom, only to find out from a neighbor who was helping her that she had been at the hospital since the night before. And we found out my grandmother suffered a heart attack and was declared dead at 1:45 a.m. the following day. My dad was declared dead at 1:45 p.m., which is why I could not reach my mom. It was then that I realized that we were going to have two funerals at the same time. I had never seen this or experienced this. I wasn't able to help my mom at this moment; it's as if all I could do was help her with my dad's funeral arrangements. But something gave me comfort, she said; she had already said goodbye to my dad in her heart because she could see his health deteriorating.

> "This hope is a strong and trustworthy anchor
> for our souls. It leads us through the curtain
> into God's inner sanctuary."
> —*Hebrews 6:19, NLT*

The part I forgot was that he was in Glory with "His Blessed Heavenly Father" (this was how my dad started his prayers). This fact was now my *hope* yet nothing had been planned. For an instant, I thought my daddy had just left. Now what? Then I remembered that I had created a Health Directive for him and had it notarized. "Those who fear the LORD are secure; he will be a refuge for their children" (Proverbs 14:26, NLT).

We just happened to be living in my bachelor's apartment at the time. That just happened to be across the street from a funeral home. You can't make this up! But even so, I felt fear and worry come over me. "Ohh, what are we going to do now?" I thought, "My Dad never had any money in his account; he always gave it away or used it for ministry." But this month, because he was sick, he was unable to withdraw it. It seemed like this was the richest he'd ever been. I remembered the name of this funeral home, called them, and they helped us. Since the convalescent home only gave us two hours to remove his body, this was literally the Grace of God that we were able to do this.

The next day, we came by to pick out a casket for my dad and prepare a memorial service for the same week. We closed his bank account with this health directive. Later on, we were able to get this money to my mom for whatever she needed, and we took part of it for the memorial expenses.

The reason everything was so fast was one: my mom had already made arrangements in Mexico, and two: we wanted those who knew my daddy here in the States to come and say goodbye. He had a great community of friends, pastors, and family who could not travel to Mexico for this. You see, he was also a missionary for the Gospel in the 80s and 90s. A story for another time. He lived and breathed the story of "The Good Samaritan" many times on the road to and from Ensenada, Mexico, even with his kids in the car. We got to witness this all the time.

And the funny part of this story is the day we did his memorial. This story was the one all of his kids could think of. It was beautiful, powerful, and amazing. The story

I shared was when I asked him, "Daddy, why do you help these people on the road, aren't you worried about our safety?" and his response was, "Mija, if I only get an hour with these folks and I get to preach the gospel to them, then I'm going to continue. It's what God calls us to do, to help others and share the gospel wherever we go."

It's Time to Leave for Mexico

The Lord helped us throughout this time by providing for us. My car was having mechanical issues, so my mother-in-law loaned us her car. Another miracle. We left that Friday. The plan was to get to Mexico as they were transporting the body. But this mortuary was amazing; they moved quickly and arrived at the funeral home connected to this cemetery in Ensenada before they got there. They held his body at the Department of Health in Mexican customs for safety measures and documentation, so there was a bit of a delay, but the Lord still showed up for us, even in this. As we are going through this, my youngest brother was helping my mom make arrangements for my grandmother's funeral as well. We had the official wake for both, followed by the burial service the following morning.

The burial was on a Sunday, and we were in the cemetery after the service. One of my brothers said to the other, "Hey, bro, Happy Father's Day," as we all realized that we were burying my dad on Father's Day. The reality hit everyone. To some, my dad was a spiritual father; to others, a mentor; to his own, he was DAD or Daddy. We all traveled after the burial to a place called the Blow Hole (La Bufadora). It was a place my dad loved going to see

God's strength. He used to say that a whale got trapped in the cave and kept trying to get out. Once in a while, if you got close to the edge, you could experience this whale trying to get out. Then, suddenly, the spray of the top of this whale would blow ocean water into your face if you weren't careful. He was a great storyteller and had everyone laughing when they realized it was just an anomaly caused by sea pressure coming out of a cave. In all our years visiting this tourist spot, we always wished we could see the whales on their migration route. On the day after the funeral, we saw a family of whales swimming north from their time in Baja. It was beautiful.

> "Let all that I am wait quietly before God, for my hope is in him. He alone is my rock and my salvation, my fortress where I will not be shaken. My victory and honor come from God alone. He is my refuge, a rock where no enemy can reach me. O my people, trust in him at all times. Pour out your heart to him, for God is our refuge. ... Common people are as worthless as a puff of wind, and the powerful are not what they appear to be. If you weigh them on the scales, together they are lighter than a breath of air."
>
> —*Psalms 62:5-9, NLT*

It's important to mourn with your loved ones

When my tears finally arrived two weeks after the burial, I woke up in the middle of the night, and a wave of emotions just came over me. I was so glad my husband was there during all of this. First, it was sorrow that my daddy would not get a chance to meet my daughter, then it became anger that he didn't take care of himself when he should've, regarding his diabetes—maybe he could've lived longer. He was always stubborn about his health. Then disbelief that he was gone. Throughout this outburst of emotions, my amazing husband was there, rubbing my back in silence, letting me pour my heart out in grief ... There is something so precious when the Healer is there. The Lord reminded me that over 300 guests attended his funeral, mourning him. This moment also brought me hope that one day I will see him again. That his Kingdom-minded life left us this beautiful example of some of the seeds he'd planted. In the realization of all this, I felt God's presence in our room as I wailed and then wept.

"He heals the brokenhearted and bandages their wounds."

—*Psalms 147:3, NLT*

This verse reminded me that's exactly what Jesus did during all of this. He will heal your broken heart and bandage your wounds. But you have to let Him. For me, letting Him meant choosing to be honest with Jesus about my pain, sometimes during quiet prayer or just allowing myself to sit in His presence even when my emotions felt overwhelming. It looked like surrendering everything I could not control and trusting that He truly cared for every ache in my heart. It wasn't always easy, but each time I took my hurts to Him, He brought comfort in His own gentle way.

Gratitude

Gratitude came slowly after that night of grieving. But I still remember these moments as if I lived them just a few weeks ago. I'm not saying I'm in mourning anymore because I've walked through my own internal healing.

During this time, I remembered a dream I had as a newlywed: my dad was rocking in a hammock in our new home, which had French doors that opened onto a dining room. A very beautiful moment: a warm glow, and time seemed to stand still. In this dream, some boxes needed to be unboxed because we had just moved into this place. My husband and his buddies were moving furniture in, and as they were doing this, I said out loud, "Hey, guys, how about some pizza?" As I go to grab the phone to order, I turn to my left into this dining room, and I see my dad laughing and holding this beautiful, perfectly happy baby girl, and she looks at me with such joy, and then the light hits her eyes, and I can see they were lavender in color. I knew at that moment that this baby was mine, and my daddy was holding her for me. I asked the Lord, "What did this dream mean?" And He said, "I give good gifts to my children, and I want to give her to you."

My daughter was born in January 2008. She just turned 18, loves art and sculpting, and has a beautiful singing voice.

My son just turned 16 at the beginning of this Hope Chapter. Still, his salvation story began with a Good Friday service, and he was baptized last year after a Winter Camp trip. Two weeks ago, I witnessed my first-born daughter's water baptism; she had already experienced salvation at 10 years old during a sunrise service at our church. It seems my life will now be marked by the death and life of Jesus through their story.

I still miss my dad from time to time, like during my kids' milestones and when my son was a baby. Sometimes his baby face reminded me of my dad. Other times, as he got older, his sense of humor. And my daughter's beautiful heart and stubbornness at times. I remember conversations I had with him. Funny stories he'd share with me about his dating life. Or miracle stories he'd share about our family.

As you read this, I invite you to pause and reflect on your own hopes for the future. What are you trusting God for in this season? If you feel comfortable, share your hopes with those around you, or even write them down to help you keep believing in them. Let us pray for each other and encourage one another to hold on to hope, knowing that God is faithful to heal us from our mourning. May our stories and prayers become a source of ongoing encouragement and community on this journey.

Throughout this experience, the verse that kept coming to mind was the one my dad would end our church services with, and we would say it with JOY. I remember it well as a little girl. There was a cadence to it in Spanish, and it sums up what we experienced in this season and what every believer will experience at some time in their own walk with Jesus: "rejoicing in hope, patient in tribulation, continuing steadfastly in prayer" (Romans 12:12, NKJV).

I love the Passion Translation:

> Let this hope burst forth within you, releasing a continual joy. Don't give up in a time of trouble, but commune with God at all times. (Romans 12:12, TPT)

We live in the enduring hope that one day we'll be reunited in Glory with my papa, my daddy, and my grandmother. I look forward with expectancy to my children's future, trusting completely in the Lord's plan for them. This hope isn't just a wish—it is rooted in the life, death, and resurrection of Jesus. Every day, I embrace His grace with a grateful heart. For all He has done, all He is doing, and all He has promised, I am filled with His peace, His joy, and the strength of His word.

Next Steps

Honoring those you are memorializing. Being prepared for the unexpected. God will meet you where you are.

Make sure to honor those you are burying and be prepared for the unexpected. God will meet you where you are. Honoring your loved ones can take many forms: you might share memories and stories of their life, gather with family and friends to recall what made them special, plant a tree or flower in their name, or give to a cause that was important to them. Acts of service, spending time in prayer, or simply taking a quiet moment to reflect can also be meaningful tributes. Or visiting a place they once liked. However you choose to honor your loved one, trust that God sees your heart and will meet you there.

It's important to mourn with your loved ones.

It's important to mourn with your loved ones. After my father's passing, on the day of his memorial, we cried and laughed as we remembered all the ways he touched our lives. Even looking at old photographs allowed us to grieve collectively. These moments of shared mourning allowed us to lean on each other and reminded me of the comfort that comes from not grieving alone.

Gratitude: Although this may be hard at first, when you are ready, and you have mourned your loved ones. Think of all of the things that make you grateful to have had this person in your life—the funny stories and memories. And give thanks to the Lord, for their life.

Prayer:

Father God, we come before you as your children. In the midst of our sorrow and pain, we turn to You, the source of our comfort and healing. We ask for Your Spirit to surround us, for Your peace to calm our troubled spirits, and for Your healing touch to mend our wounded hearts. Jesus, shine Your light of Hope in the darkness of grief, and may Your love carry us through this time. We thank You for the process of grieving. Because it teaches us to sit still, it allows our souls to heal. Jesus, You took all of our griefs upon you here on earth and on the cross. So that we would one day walk with Hope in our own lives, in our families, and in our future with You. Hebrews 6:19 says, "This hope we have as an anchor of the soul, both sure and steadfast" (NKJV). And Lord, we know that in Hebrew the word for Hope is Tikvah, a secure lifeline to hold on to. Will You be the lifeline that we need in this hour? Will you stay close to Your children during this time for those who may be grieving? We come against the lies that we are not allowed to grieve, in Jesus name. I thank You for the Healing through Your Spirit. In the midst of our Grief, we place our trust in Your loving big arms, knowing and trusting that You are our refuge and our healer. "My health may fail, and my spirit may grow weak, but God remains the strength of my heart; he is mine forever" (Psalms 73:26, NLT).

Holy Spirit, You are our strength and our portion forever, "Blessed are they that mourn: for they shall be comforted" (Matthew 5:4, KJV). You are our comforter. In Jesus' name we pray, AMEN.

When I Grow Up

By Charlotte Hammett Hubrich

It all started during my junior year of high school. One summer day, my dad walked through the family room and found my sister and me watching *Days of Our Lives*, a daytime drama on television.

He saw an actress emoting, looked at me, and quietly said, "You could do that!"

That was it—I was hooked! So, when adults asked me what I wanted to be when I grew up, I proudly said, "I want to be an actress. "

I have since realized that I not only loved my dad but also wanted him to be proud of me. So that appraisal of my talent stuck with me and directed much of my life from my early twenties to my early forties.

At the time, I did not understand that I was trying to prove my worth through a gift that my dad had recognized.

Is there a dream from your early childhood that has stayed with you? Is it your own dream or one suggested to you? Has that dream been realized? Or did you dream a new dream?

Are you doing today what you thought you would be doing when you were younger? How would you answer, "What do you want to be when you grow up?"

Regardless of where you are in your quest for dreams to come true or goals to be reached, do you have a plan for a timeline?

I stuck with my dream of being an actress for almost twenty years. Little did I know that pursuing what I thought I wanted in life could bring such disappointment and hurt.

It did not start out in disappointment. In fact, I took my love of acting to college and earned both a Bachelor's and a Master's degree in Speech and Theatre. I enjoyed leading roles in plays in undergraduate school, such as Laura in Ketti Fring's play, *Look Homeward Angel,* based on the novel by Thomas Wolfe. I also played the Narrator as Jack in the Box in *Aesop's Fables.* My favorite role was Nancy in *Oliver,* the book and music by Lionel Hart, based on the novel by Charles Dickens.

After I received my Master's, I was hired by a college in a small town near my hometown. I liked teaching, working with students, and directing young talent in plays such as Noel Cowerd's *Blithe Spirit* and *God's Favorite,* Neil Simon's modern take on the trials of Job in the Old Testament.

I was, however, bored with the small town life, and I still had acting ambitions of my own.

That is when the voice of discontentment began to whisper, "You need to get out of this town." The college town offered no restaurants, no museums, no theatres to see shows, no theatre companies to audition for. I was bored!

While boredom seems innocent enough, it can certainly lead to distraction, which leads to bad decisions. Even though I was happy at the college itself, I began searching for new work. I read that a local television station in a larger city not far from the college was looking for weekend weather anchors. For some reason, I thought that I was their girl.

It turns out that after I auditioned for the weekend job, I was their girl. I could have easily kept my day job at the college and commuted on weekends to do the weather, but oh no, I had to go at it—"all or nothing!"

I resigned from the college and off down the road I drove toward stardom.

I wanted to be an actress! And I was an actress, alright! I certainly was not a meteorologist! I talked about the weather before you had to have a degree in meteorology to talk about cold and warm fronts.

I could see, though, that I would have to study meteorology if I were to advance in this career. After one summer course in Meteorology, I found out quickly that my brain was not wired for science. After some struggles with angst and despair over this realization, I ended my time on air discussing the weather.

Still, the drive to fulfill my childhood dream to be an actress haunted me. While I thought that I was using my God-given talent, I later realized that I was trying to prove my worth by stacking up achievements. I did not accept myself without the next checkmark of achievement.

After I gave up being a weekend weather anchor, I saw a story about a repertory theatre company at the University of Louisville. It was located in Louisville, Kentucky, our state's largest city. I called and asked if I could audition for their program. The doors opened wide.

I auditioned for and received a three-year scholarship to study acting and get my MFA in Acting—no cost to me, except time and effort!

I excelled there. I became a part of the repertory company that I had seen advertised. I had the opportunity to travel locally with the repertory company and do roles like Laura in Tennessee Williams's *Glass Menagerie* and Queen Eurydice in the Greek tragedy *Antigone.*

In addition to the repertory company, I was also cast in many lead roles. I had the opportunity to play Nora in Henrik Ibsen's *A Doll's House.* As Nora, I found catharsis in being able to tell her emotionally abusive husband goodbye. The other cathartic role for me was Babe in *Crimes of the Heart* by Beth Henley. One of my favorite scenes shows Babe having a particularly bad day. Her sister, Meg, comes in and finds Babe with her head in the oven. Babe tells her sister, "I had a bad day, Meg, I had a really bad day." I resonated with my character's bad day. While I never considered ending my life, I did drive myself to distraction and depression.

Successes at the university boosted my confidence; however, it also fed my ambition. The ambition was like an addiction to approval and accomplishment. The more I accomplished, the more I needed to continue working my way up in the ranks of whatever the highest reward was that the actor/actress world could afford me. At this time, I was blind to the fact that I had made acting my "god."

I would soon learn one of my first important life lessons—My whole self-worth was dependent on who chose me for the next major accomplishment. I falsely believed that I was in the will of God. I was not, however, listening to God. I had an elevated sense of self and did things my way.

While a part of me knew that I should *not* judge my self-worth by how many commercial spots I got on television or how many lead roles I had, I still struggled to let go and let God lead me.

At this point in time, I was still holding on to control. After I graduated from grad school, where I had many lead roles, I was hired by a professional repertory company in another state. That was a huge accomplishment! God blessed me with that opportunity or allowed me to have it. What I did with the opportunity was up to me, right?

Well, I spent a torturous year at the professional company. Another major life lesson came when I woke up to the fact that I was looking through a distorted lens. I was slowly learning that my negative thinking was helping to create both negative feelings and experiences.

In hindsight, it wasn't that bad! The nagging thoughts that ruled my mind about the experience made it unbearable for me. I gave in to the temptation to lean on the thoughts that fooled me and temporarily defeated me.

Even though I had been hired to be a part of the Shakespearean company to tour the schools, the discontented voice whispered again, "You need more than touring to schools. You need to get on the main stage." I concluded that I wasn't good enough until I got on the Main Stage—here I was again—always looking for the next achievement!

Even though I made it to the main stage in Jane Martin's *Talking With* and Agatha Christie's *Mouse Trap*, I did not like the competition or the interminable amount of time it took to get there. You could equate this drive to the determination to get a promotion or a raise. I entertained the false idea that nothing was ever enough. I was miserable, and I needed a change.

In the height of depression, I started to learn two lessons almost simultaneously.

The first lesson that crystallized for me was that the need for constant approval and advancement was not making me happy. The adoration was a temporary anecdote to low self-worth or self-esteem. Concurrently, I was figuring out through Scripture reading, prayer, and therapy with a Christian counselor that life could be filled with joy again. My current state of negative, 'never enough' thinking was helping to create negative experiences. Not only did I make bad career choices, but I also made hurtful relationship choices. Both caused me a world of pain. My negative thinking led to choices that were destructive to my emotional, mental, and spiritual health.

Thank God for more chances. I experienced a turnaround when one of my family members reminded me of Romans 5:8. It reads, "But God demonstrates his love for us in this: While we were still sinners, Christ died for us" (NIV). I did not have to keep stacking up achievements— God loves me just as I am. My hope and peace were restored when I woke up and started to believe that God loved me unconditionally.

I wish I could say that I learned this right away. It took me a while to fully realize the extent of God's love and acceptance.

I had to hit bottom, however, to have that "Aha." What I did realize through God's grace was that my thoughts and my behavior were not making me happy. I was not finding peace in the world until I returned to Jesus.

From childhood, I learned about God and understood that God sent his son, Jesus, to earth in human form to reconcile God to the brokenness of humanity.

Why had I forgotten that God loved me just as I was? I didn't have to prove anything to Him. My dad didn't want me to prove anything to him either. I feel sure that even though he inadvertently planted the acting seed in my head, he would have rejoiced if I had quit acting sooner than I did. I do want to clarify that acting is not bad in and of itself. It was just not a good fit for me. No one else was responsible for my decisions except me.

I am so grateful that I returned to what I had learned as a child. The most important lesson I remembered was the unconditional love of God.

In my late thirties, early forties, I started to change my thoughts with God's help. One, I remembered God's unconditional love. I asked Him to forgive my wayward path of trying to do things on my own. Second, I asked Him to heal my thinking.

Through prayer and reading Scripture, I experienced a newfound awareness when I revisited one of my favorite Bible verses. Romans 12:2 (KJV) reads, "And be not conformed to this world: but be ye transformed by the renewing of your mind, that ye may prove what is that good, acceptable, and perfect, will of God."

I keep 2 Timothy 1:7 (KJV) close by me to this day. When I get afraid that I am not enough or that something terrible could happen, I read and meditate on it: "For God hath not given us a spirit of fear, but of power, and of love, and of a sound mind."

These life lessons are so critical to my peace of mind—God loves me unconditionally and does not plant fear. Fear is of the enemy. God's way is one of power, love, and a *sound mind.*

As a pastor's kid, I had been given the blueprint to be happy in Jesus. Both of my parents loved the Lord and taught me to do the same. While Jesus became a part of my life, I still clung to earthly goals. I was living in and for this world and what I could get out of it. I thought for a long time that I was just following a goal, a dream. I was, however, *in the world and of the world.*

So, "the way of the world" was the road I traveled from my mid twenties to mid forties. During those twenty years, I rationalized thoughts like, "Didn't God want me to use my gifts?"

My hope came during my retirement from teaching college. I felt the Lord urging me to use my gifts for Him. I sensed Him saying, "You have acted, you have spoken to students, you have spoken in workshops, NOW speak for me.

I have talked a great deal about my ambitions. We all have different ambitions—dreams for which we strive. It is healthy to have goals. I learned, though, that making goals my 'god,' was not only sinful, it was detrimental to my health—physical, mental, and spiritual. Only when I sought the Lord's guidance did I begin to experience peace. Believe me, you won't find peace in the world—only in the Word!

Nothing could compare with His unconditional love and acceptance, which transformed and renewed my mind. I was waking up to the fact that I had been miserable because all of the praise from others could not fill the emptiness in my heart and mind.

The quest for love and acceptance apart from what God had already provided was futile! The Bible says that God loves and accepts us as we are. We read in Romans 5:8, "But God demonstrates his own love for us in this: While we were still sinners, Christ died for us" (NIV). Christ made the ultimate sacrifice while we were still sinners. He loved us even while we were off on our own wayward path.

We can all get lured into false thinking: "If I can just get this goal met or be accepted by this group of people, or if my children can just succeed in their school, career, and personal choices." Peace will not come from trying to make things happen. Peace only comes from asking for the Lord's guidance.

The third life lesson for me was one of surrender. Surrender continues to challenge me sometimes. I trust that God had been preparing me to surrender to Him. He did this first by reminding me to accept His unconditional love for me, and second, He prepared my heart to ask Him to create in me a sound mind and heart. I no longer desired to live without His precious direction.

After enough pain, I finally surrendered and asked God to take charge of my life. I asked Him to help me because I had made a mess of things on my own. I realized that the emptiness I tried to fill with acting and poor relationship choices only brought chaos and despair. I could only find peace and love in the one Jesus offered me. Can you believe that I was too stubborn to receive His gift of peace and unconditional love? My failed relationships and career disappointments showed me that success and ambition weren't foolproof. Only Jesus could pick up the pieces of my shattered dreams and broken heart.

So, it was time for a change. I abdicated my control to the love of Jesus. One cold winter night, I stood in front of my house and begged God to take my *desperation to act* away from me. I can still feel the release from that attachment. At age 44, I felt the same lightness that I had felt as a child. For now, I was willing to fully be a child of God.

My plans without God's guidance took me down many lonely and desperate roads. When I returned to a sound mind in Christ, I trusted God again and wanted Him to lead.

Jeremiah 29:11 says, "'For I know the plans I have for you,' declares the Lord, 'plans to prosper you and not to harm you, plans to give you hope and a future'" (NIV). A future with God is not full of chaos and despair. I realized that I no longer wanted to be in chaos, so I invited Jesus to take charge. He provided peace and contentment and eradicated my chaos and despair.

He offers the same peace and contentment to you, too, in your place where life hasn't gone as you planned. Your story of striving for approval is most likely different from mine. There is no amount of fame, fortune, or approval that fills the emptiness in our lives other than a relationship with Jesus.

When I asked God to take away my addiction to acting and replace it with the joy and love of Christ, I like to say that I returned to sanity.

With a sound mind in Christ, He eventually led me to my current husband. At age 46, I was introduced to a widower who also had a relationship with Jesus Christ. We married, and I have the additional joy, love, and acceptance from him and our shared love for Jesus. In addition to my husband of twenty-six years, God also directed me toward a new career. I was hired by another college to teach speech and communication. I wondered for a long time why God closed the theatre door, but I found myself very content and fulfilled teaching speech and communication. This time, I stayed at the college, and I taught for thirty-one years as opposed to my first teaching experience of a two-year stay. When I rested in God's best plans for me rather than striving on my own, I felt a divine joy, love, and peace that only came through the presence of Jesus Christ in my life.

C. S. Lewis is one of my favorite authors. His famous quote from *Mere Christianity* helped me to stop directing my life: "Give up yourself, and you will find yourself, and you will find your real self. Submit to death, the death of your ambitions and favorite wishes every day. Submit to the death of your whole body. Submit with every fiber of your being, and you will find eternal life."[8] Lewis's words reflect the teaching of Jesus, in Matthew 16:25, " For whoever wants to save their life will lose it, but whoever loses their life for me will find it" (NIV).

Finally, I was waking up. When I died to what I thought I wanted and allowed God to guide me, I found joy in my life. God took my selfish striving that caused chaos and despair and replaced them with peace of mind and contentment. Joy and peace came in the form of a husband and career that brought just that and more! If you're experiencing strife and chaos, there's a better way to receive what you desire in life. Jesus takes your passion and desires and aligns them with his best plan. A life with Christ isn't about giving up things; it's about God transforming you to be more like him. 1 John 1:9 affirms, " If we confess our sins, God is faithful and just and will forgive us our sins and purify us from all unrighteousness" (NIV). That's what God did when I accepted him into my life and started giving

---

8   Lewis, C. S. *Mere Christianity.* Samizdat, 2014, 120.

up my self-seeking ways to God's peace and control. My priorities began to change. I no longer had to strive for acceptance and joy. It was there with Christ as the director and shepherd of my life.

I had finally accepted 2 Corinthians 5:17: " Therefore, if anyone is in Christ, the new creation has come. The old has gone, the new is here!" (NIV). My new life looks like a loving and devoted husband. I retired from a successful teaching career, which was more suited to my need for stability both in work and at home. Now, in retirement, I have answered God's call to speak for Him. God blessed me with the opportunity to become a certified Stonecroft speaker. Stonecroft is a non-denominational, non -profit Christian organization that prepares women to lead Christian groups within their communities. It has been my pleasure to speak regionally to Christian Women Connection groups. I now serve as Kentucky's Regional Speaker trainer to help other women construct their stories of redemption and restoration. You can also rest in redemption and restoration.

Next Steps

First, I encourage you to accept the unconditional love of a caring God who sent His son, Jesus, to wash away your sins. When we all realize that His sacrifice covers our waywardness and sin, we can accept the forgiveness he offers. No longer will you have to prove yourself. You can just *be* yourself in Christ.

Second, allow God's word to heal your mind. Be willing to be transformed by the renewing of your mind as Scripture instructs. I found great help through prayer, meditation on

God's word, and small group Bible studies. You may find, as I did, that you need the guidance of a trusted pastor or Christian counselor.

Finally, surrender your life, your worries, your dreams, and your goals to a loving Father. God's word is here to guide you to your best life, not the life of the ego, but the life of true peace and happiness in Christ. Until I did this part, peace evaded me. Now, peace abides.

I still have to surrender daily. It may not be easy, but it gets easier because that surrender is not just me; it is Christ in me.

Glory be to God for more chances to keep growing and to finally grow up in Christ.

*

About the
Authors

Ramela G. Abbamontian

amela Grigorian Abbamontian, PhD, is an art historian and college professor passionate about art's power to enrich lived experience. A connector and encourager at heart, she creates spaces that bring people together and foster community. With a heart for service, she is active in ministries at The Mount Bible Church. She enjoys visiting museums, theater, and traveling with her family. A Revelation Wellness Instructor, she is committed to whole-person wellness rooted in faith. As a cancer survivor and caregiver, she shares hope through her writing. She lives in Los Angeles with her husband Jimmy and daughters Grace, Lily, and Ella.

Instagram: https://www.instagram.com/ramelaabba/

Email: ramelaabbamontian@gmail.com

Ericka Reid

Ericka Reid, Ph.D., M.Ed. currently works for a national research institute dedicated to public health and service. She is also an educational psychologist and personal development specialist who helps women in midlife navigate change with clarity and confidence. She supports them in redefining who they are, releasing what no longer fits, and choosing lives aligned with their truth. Her work blends insight with practical tools to help women move forward with purpose. Through coaching, teaching, and writing, she encourages women to trust themselves, honor their journeys, and embrace what's next. Based in North Carolina's Triangle area, Ericka enjoys creative pursuits, brunching, yoga, kickboxing, and loving on her senior Shihpoo, Lucy Pearl.

Website: www.erickareidphd.com

Stacey Gawthrop

Stacey Gawthrop is a wife, mother of six (two of whom were adopted), and Gigi to 3 grandchildren. She currently resides in San Antonio, Texas, with her husband of 37 years. She has published articles in Guideposts and Christiandevotions.us. She loves to help gather and connect people to one another and share the heart of the Father.

Facebook: facebook.com@Stacey Gawthrop

Katherine Freeman

Katherine Freeman is currently working at the University of Illinois and lives with her husband in Monticello, Illinois. She holds a Bachelor's degree in Speech and Theatre from the University of Oregon and a Master's in Educational Policy and Leadership from the University of Illinois. In her free time, she enjoys writing, directing, quilting, watercolor painting, and spending time with her husband, father, children, granddaughter, and friends.

"Keep your heart with all diligence, for out of
it spring the issues of life."
—*Proverbs 4:23, NKJV*

Lindsay Koach

Lindsay is a wife and mother of three children, an Integrative Nutrition Health Coach, and a Naturopathic Practitioner specializing in women's thyroid and hormone health. She was born and raised and resides with her family in Ellwood City, Pennsylvania. In addition to her online health coaching offerings on heal.me/heartspeakhealth, she provides a free hypothyroidism support group on Facebook called "Hypothyroidism Support: Alternative Solutions for Thyroid & Hormone Health." Lindsay contributed to *A Peaceful New Year* in 2025 with Hope Books. You can find articles and written works on her website heartspeakhealth.com.

Website: https://www.heartspeakhealth.com

Facebook: https://www.facebook.com/heartspeakhealth

Instagram: https://www.instagram.com/heartspeakhealth

Melanie Wamoff

Melanie Wamhoff is passionate about growing in her understanding of the Bible and sharing it with women. For nearly 30 years, she has been teaching women's Bible studies or Sunday School classes. She also speaks about supporting friends through infertility, miscarriage, and stillbirth, and discipling children. She loves encouraging people to share testimonies of God's faithfulness in their lives. Now that her four children are grown and their homeschooling is complete, she is devoting her time to writing her own testimonies and Bible studies. Melanie and her husband reside near Omaha, Nebraska, not too far from their four grandchildren.

Instagram: https://www.instagram.com/melaniewbooks

Website: www.theentirestory.org

Anna Gall

*A*nna Gall's works are published in eMerge, Persimmon Tree, and Flapper Press, and her poem, Seashells is included in the anthology *Dairy Hollow Echo*. In 2025, Anna published her memoir as a culinary professional in a two-volume book, *Strewn Words in the Stew: A Memoir of Poems, Short Stories, and Sayings*. These books are filled with her original recipes, photos, poems, and short stories. The author resides in St. Charles, Missouri, with her husband. They have six grown children, nine grandchildren, and one great-grandchild. In her spare time, Anna finds joy in cooking, gardening, antiques, music, and traveling.

Website: https://deannagreensandgardenart.com

Blog: https://womanwarrior.blog

Elisa Rendon

Elisa Rendon is the author of the book *Deliverance from Fear*, published in December, 2021. She lives with her daughter in Ridgefield Park, New Jersey. Born in Cuba, she came to the United States at eleven years of age. She obtained both a Bachelor's and a Master's degree in English from Rutgers University, Newark, New Jersey.

She's the happy grandmother of two boys, a 22-month-old and a newborn. Her son, Mark, is the proud father. He currently works as an EMT, with the ultimate goal of being a firefighter. Her daughter Melissa lives with her in Ridgefield Park and is currently studying at Montclair University to become a forensic psychologist.

Elisa attends the Northern New Jersey Vineyard church in South Hackensack, New Jersey.

Email: rendonelisa905@gmail.com.

Noemi Rivas

Noemi Solis Rivas, an Intercessor at her church, volunteers in all areas of the ministry of healing, loves Father God, Jesus, and her best friend, the Holy Spirit. She is a wife married to her amazing husband for 20 years, and a mom to two beautiful teens. She desires that others would come to know Jesus through her stories of healing, salvation, and restoration.

Charlotte Hubrich

Charlotte Hammett Hubrich is a speaker, facilitator, and educator. Charlotte is a certified speaker for Stonecroft Ministries and serves as her State's Speaker Trainer for Stonecroft. She enjoys speaking to Christian Women's groups in her region: Kentucky, Indiana, Illinois, and Tennessee.

Charlotte is registered with ChristianWomenSpeakers.com.

She holds a Master's degree in Speech and Theatre from Western KY University and a Master of Fine Arts in Acting from the University of Louisville. She spent some time in professional theater but found her true love was teaching. She is a retired associate professor of Communication at Jefferson Community and Technical College, where she taught for thirty-one years.

Charlotte and her husband enjoy gardening and traveling. She is a step-mother and grandmother.

Website: www.yourarmorofgod.com

LinkedIn: www.linkedin.com/in/charlottehubrich

Website: www.womenspeakers.com

Closing

Dear Reader,

Thank you for reading *My Hope Story Vol. 3*!

I want to take a moment to celebrate the incredible authors who contributed to this meaningful book. They have poured their hearts into discovering, clarifying, and sharing their unique messages—and now, you get to benefit from their hard work and dedication.

At hope*books, we are deeply proud of our authors and are honored to partner with them on this journey. If you've ever considered writing and publishing your book, we invite you to visit hopebooks.com to learn more about our coaching and publishing services. We believe that everyone has a message to share and an audience to serve, and the world needs your hopeful words now more than ever.

Once again, let's take a moment to celebrate the hard work of these authors in bringing *My Hope Story Vol. 3* to life.

Sincerely,

Brian Dixon

Publisher, hope*books

Looking to *connect* with a community of writers?

hope✳writers

www.hopewriters.com 

> The world needs your *hope-filled* words more now than ever before.

Thinking about *writing* your own book?

 hope✳books

www.hopebooks.com